T0147607

UNSHELTERED

I've Been Through the Fire and I've Come Out Pure Gold

L'trece Ann Worsham

iUniverse, Inc.
New York   Bloomington

Unsheltered
I've Been Through the Fire and
I've Come Out Pure Gold

iUniverse books may be ordered through booksellers or by contacting:

iUniverse
1663 Liberty Drive
Bloomington, IN 47403
www.iuniverse.com
1-800-Authors (1-800-288-4677)

ISBN: 978-1-4502-4663-7 (sc)
ISBN: 978-1-4502-4664-4 (ebook)

Printed in the United States of America

iUniverse rev. date: 8/3/2010

Contents

Chapter 1 (Rough Start)

1969, There was a woman named Rosa B. Tiller, who gave birth to some twelve healthy children. For some unknown reason she really took favor to her baby girls' first born of four. This first born child named L'trece Ann Worsham was later known as Trece Ann; and that girl is me. The very day I was born, just fresh out of the womb, my grandmother Rosa B. noticed that my skin felt like beach sand was all over me. It later came to be known that I was born with a could be crippling skin disease that was not only painful, itchy and infectious, but during infectious episodes it could be contagious. Due to this rare skin disease and my mother being so young, my grandmother decided to help my mother with my care. My mother Minnie Mae Tiller (Peewee) was pretty much inexperienced and would cry every time I cried. She could not understand why I was crying all the time. No body knew that it came from my fathers side of the family. His whole family has this disease. It almost drove my aunt Joan crazy. She was covered with this disease and it is very noticeable causing great embarrassment. My fathers mother was also covered and people would stare and make faces and even rude comments. As a child these things are emotionally damaging. It causes you to wear clothing not suitable to the weather like long clothing in the summertime just to keep people from knowing that your skin is so discolored and thick and rough that I didn't want any one to see my skin. Some times it gets so dry that it breaks open and that really hurts. It burns while your in the shower. It blisters and leaks when it's infected and it's extremely itchy and flaky. When its flaky and itchy and I scratch it, the flakes fall off and covers your bed sheets at night while you sleep. Then when I sweat it burns. The disease also comes with allergies and is triggered by stress. The allergies included poultry, seafood, dairy products, tobacco, roaches and some other things that I can't quite remember. We did not know that until after I became an adult so I was always going through this torture and it got worse every time someone had an idea of how to cure me. I went through a lot of home remedies which sometimes irritated my skin even worse because my mother could not afford proper medical treatment. A lot of times during the hot summer months while all the other kids were happy and playing outside I would be in tears because the heat was pure torture for me. My own sweat would cause uncontrollable itching and burning which in turn would lead to thick, puss leaking sores on my neck, arms, legs , feet and hands. The sores became infected and caused my glands to swell which in turn made it very hard to walk. I had to walk on my toes because my legs were stuck in a bent position. My cousins would pick on me and say things like she's walking on invisible high heel shoes. Other kids used to pick on the discoloration of my skin and that was due to beach water. By one of the allergies associated with this disease being seafood, then common sense should have told them that beach water was no good. They thought it would help me but the salt only burned and made it worse. Doctors wanted to give me a blood transfusion but my mom said no.

They even wanted to amputate my big toe one time because it was so infected that it looked like it was decaying. My mother said no to that also and they gave me an injection of cortizone and my toe came back to normal. There is no cure for this disease therefore I will suffer this disease for the rest of my life with only minor ways of keeping it under control.

Chapter 2 (spare the rod and spoil the child)

My grandmother decided to raise me for a while because my dad had been forced to move away and leave me and my mom. My stay with my grandmother lasted six years until the day I said I wanted to go home. During the time I was with my grandmother, we went everywhere the church went. My grandmother was a good God fearing woman. She attended church functions three to four times a week and sometimes we would go out of town to fellowship with other churches. All of her friends would say "there's that little Treceann," and after church there would be long tables of food with everything from fried chicken to lemon cake. All kinds of pies and soft drinks. The children would hurry and eat so we could go out back and play with little spoons and pots and pans pretending we were cooks ourselves. Every now and then one of us had to get a spanking for some reason or another. It was either getting caught playing in the water spicket or climbing on top of the house. My cousin Lynn got a spanking one time because she called my grandmothers food mess. We all knew to eat whatever she put on your plate and don't say anything except thank you . Every body except Lynn. She was more rebellious than the rest of us. But those were the good old days when kids respected their elders. My grandmother believed that if you spared the rod that you spoiled the child. So, whatever you did you got your spanking right then not later, unless it was in church when you misbehaved. My grandmother enforced strict rules in church and you had better abide by them or else. But most of the time when all of us would get together it was most definitely going to be trouble. We weren't allowed to turn our heads to look back at the door when someone entered or she would escort you outside and around to the back of the church, get some switches and spank us silly. I remember getting slapped in church for laughing during the time some one else was reading in Sunday school. If you make grandma mad enough that's exactly what would happen. Most of the slaps came from us falling asleep while the pastor was preaching when grandma felt like we should be listening. It seemed wrong at the time but it kept kids in order. I most definitely knew the rules very well because I was living with my grandmother for my first six years. Every time my cousins came over I was tempted to crack and make jokes about the little old lady's and men in the church which caused the rest of us to laugh out loud and then everybody had to get the switch. I got a spanking one time while I was asleep. All I did was lift my leg to the back of the couch which caused my legs to be apart and she woke me up with a switch because she said I opened my legs. Under no circumstances do little girls open their legs. Even when I'd be out side playing and sometimes a little boy named Lajuan would walk by my grandmothers house and although I knew him she would say "you stay away from that Lajuan! Treceann, do you hear me?" and I would say "yes ma'am." I never could understand why all of that was so important until I grew up and started having sex. Then I understood why she never wanted us to open our legs or why she never allowed us to sit on a man's lap. She always said you never know what a man is thinking.

Chapter 3 (The Death of my Sister Dee Dee)

My mother found a very loving man after my dad left her and his name was TeeRone, and I loved him dearly, because he was very good to me and my mom , but he was a kleptomaniac. In fact he stole so much I remember a man named nee-nee putting a gun to my mother's head while she was holding my hand. We were on our way into the store when he came out of nowhere and put a long silver barrel, pearl handle gun in my mother's face and told her to tell your man "I want my shit". That man's face and gun stained my memory forever. My mother had given birth to a daughter from TeeRone, but she died at the age of six months. At that time I was about 4 or 5 years old, and I remember going into her room watching her and rubbing her fingers as she slept. I did this routinely every night and morning when I was there; then one day she just wasn't there anymore. That was a very sad day for all of us. The doctor's said that she simply forgot to breath and they called it crib death. It was a very trying time and after the funeral I don't think my mother or TeeRone could bear to be together anymore. They went there separate ways

Chapter 4 (moving away)

By the time I was Eight years old we moved to Dayton, Ohio with a man we barely knew. My mother met him and almost immediately, she fell in love with him. His name was Tommy Lee and we called him T.L. for short. She loved him so much that she trusted him enough to leave the safety of her family and go to this far away place with no means of transportation and without any money. When we finally got there It was beautiful. The climate was so much more healthier and cleaner that when you inhaled, it was truly a breath of fresh air. I used to come outside and just take in deep breaths of crisp clean air and pretend I was breathing clouds or at least that's how it seemed to me. I definitely noticed the difference in the climate. It appeared that everything was blanketed with a blinding bright white cover of snow. The snow was very cold and it took some getting used to. The greatest thing about the climate is that it was good for my skin and hair. After a few weeks my skin was beautiful and clear and I never had to use medication or go to the doctor the entire time that we lived there. It was amazing. My hair grew longer and became more manageable and it even flowed back and forth in the wind. T.L. noticed it first and he would say "look at that girls hair, boy she's looking like a movie star! Look at her face peewee," he'd say to my mom. It was pretty. My hair and skin never looked like this in Florida, so that was a good thing. I didn't even have to go to the doctor anymore. Not once in the whole time that we lived there did I have an out break. I was beautiful. We were happy at that time in our lives and my mom and I spent a lot of time together. We used to play cards together a lot and she always made sure that I had the hottest new toys. She taught me how to play spades, gin rummy ,solitaire and tunk. Then The happiness came to an end when she became pregnant. During the pregnancy T.L. left us. He just up and left us there with no warning and no way of getting help. We didn't even have much food but my mother made miracle meals out of what she had. I remember my mother walking me to school each day in the freezing snow. I was about four feet tall maybe and the snow would come almost to my waist. That was a lot to me. I hated walking in the snow when other kids loved it. I guess they were used to it, but I was not. My mother used to try and look happy on those long cold walks but I could always see the sadness through her smile. Sometimes I'd see her tears and I would ask "are you crying mama?" and she would always say "no, that's just the cold wind blowing in my eyes making them water, that's all baby." Some how I knew that it wasn't all together true but I wanted her to think I believed her even when I didn't. I hated that man making my mama sad all the time and I wondered why my daddy couldn't just come get us take us back to live with him forever. Then just out of the blue one day T.L. just came home. I remember waking up one cold and snowy day to the faint sound of my mom screaming and yelling but she wasn't in the house. I followed the sound to the huge window in the living room and when I looked out I saw my mother and him knee deep in snow fighting. He was punching her and trying to kick her and she was screaming and running and trying to fight him off at the same time. I was afraid that he was going to make her loose the baby, but she didn't. I felt helpless. If I was a man I know I would probably have killed him. Shortly after that two of my moms brothers came and moved us back to Daytona Beach. I was happy to be going back home.

Chapter 5 (Reunited
With my Cousins)

When we got back the first family members we saw were my aunt Lillie Mae and her seven kids. My Aunt Lillie Mae was a strong and stern woman. She was very dark skinned and she was a heavy set woman before dieting. She was mean when she needed to be but she was also funny. She was six years older than my mom so she pretty much told my mom what to do. She had seven kids and a lot of nieces and nephews who loved to stay with her kids. Her kids names from oldest to youngest is Poppa, a boy who is constantly playing and roughhousing any family member who comes within two feet of him no matter if it is his aunt, sister, brother, or cousin. He made every body hesitant about walking any where near him. Then it was Michelle, the oldest girl and the one with the most responsibility. Michelle got whooped for everything that everyone else did, so it made her the strongest in the long run. Michelle was short and light skinned and able to fix any thing. We called her ms. Fixit or cricket lip when ever we were mad at her because her top lip would always go the opposite way from the bottom lip. Michelle fixed all the bicycles in the neighborhood and she could fight the best which made us jealous so we started calling her a tom boy. Karen, is the one who loved for me to stay over so that she could eat my food because I was never a big eater. Karen is a very loving person who wouldn't hurt a fly, but she was more overweight than the rest of us so just because she loved to eat we called her fat mama when we were mad at her. Daphne, was the one who made every body laugh no matter what was going on. She had a sense of humor that was stewed to perfection. She would crack jokes on you so hard that even the toughest kid would cry. Daphne also had a way of making every one to be around her. She had an open mind and a free spirit and that alone mad every one want to spend the night at Aunt Lillie Mae's house. Lynn, was a more serious type and she rarely joked with us. Some times she would but most of the time she was insulted by our cracks and would go off to herself. She spent a lot of time either to herself or with friends that shared certain school events with her. Since her feelings were so easily hurt we had to watch what we said around her. Red, was always aggravating people and running away because no body could catch him. He used to steal stuff from any one who left any thing of value lying around. Then after he had stolen something from you he would help you look for it. That used to make us so mad that we would call him a sissy or a fag because red used to dress up in my aunt's clothes, shoes, make-up and wigs when no body was looking. When were all out side playing he'd sneak in the house and start dressing up. Then when we noticed his absence and went to look for him we would either catch him in the mirror dressed like a woman prancing back and forth. And last but not least my cousin Mann. Mann was only about 3-4 years old and he was jet black and he was the snitch. He was a shiny black so we called him either Sambo or Reverend

Dusty. Mann used to tell on every one else when my aunt took him to Dairy Queen. That was her way of getting all the information she wanted about what went on when she wasn't there. So as soon as Mann got that ice cream everything he promised not to tell came out. That's when the name calling would start. My aunt Lillie Mae would get so mad when we called him names but it was so funny. We had so much to talk about that night when we got back from Dayton, Oh. We were up all night having so much fun we probably didn't wake up until the next afternoon. I had acquired an accent and all my cousins were teasing me about it. I hadn't even noticed so I was not aware of it. I thought I sound the same. They said that I was talking like I was a white person. I was more advanced in school because the school work up north is more advanced than the school work here. I already knew everything they were teaching in class because I had already passed that stuff. Kids like to pick on you if they feel that you're too smart, but you don't really have to be too smart just smarter than they are.

Chapter 6 (Hot summers)

My mom soon gave birth to my little sister who was seven years younger than I. She named her Tammy Latrelle Lee. I was very happy to have a little sister but I couldn't really play with her like I wanted to, so I spent a lot of time out to my aunt's house with all my cousins cause they were always doing something fun. Sometimes we'd play kickball or four square or timeout. Sometimes we would just sit on the tank and talk. The tank was a big medal box that was big enough for at least six girls to sit on. The tank sat right at the foot of my aunt's yard, and we would sit there and watch everything on the street. We never knew exactly what the tank was but we used it for a seat if you could get there fast enough. Everyone else would just crowd around it and stand. It was just a hangout for us cause no one could actually hang out yet, we were still young. Our neighborhood was a busy one, there was always children playing. Some on their bikes, some on skates, some playing hide and go seek or like me and my cousin Daphne we were always doing gymnastics. We loved flipping around. Forward walkovers, backward walkovers, cartwheels and splits were our specialty. Back then the summers where extremely hot and when we got bored we'd just run through the ditches and the canals to cool off. Sometimes we would hunt what we called crawdads or some people call them crayfish. One day I decided to take my shoes off and play in the ditch. We were deep in the woods and while running through the ditch I cut my foot on a huge piece of glass. The cut was deep and long and we were scared cause we weren't supposed to be in the woods anyway. My cousin Michelle was more afraid than any of us cause she was the oldest and the one in charge. She was always the one to get spanking for everyone else, especially the little ones. They all got together and carried me home and bandaged me up before our parents came. The most of our troubles were with the next door neighbors. Every time their cousins from out of town came, they just had to start up a fight with us. These people were wild dirty and strong. They had two teenage cousins who were bigger and older than us. They used to sniff gas from the gas tank of their cars using water hoses and think that they were getting high. Those two were always the ones who would come into our house and tear things up and chase us all into my aunts back bathroom because we were too afraid to fight back. I remember once while we all were locked in the bathroom at one time, crying and scared to move, they pulled the water hose from outside through our living room window and simply turned it on and walked away. We stayed in that bathroom a long time waiting for them to leave and By the time we realized they were gone and what they had done it was too late, the house was flooded. My aunt was furious when she came home to that mess. She told us we better not run anymore or she would beat us herself. She told us that we had all better fight together and so we stood together from then on. Some summers were better than others, like when we went to visit our grandmothers sister in Georgia. Her name was Aunt Mae. She had all the fruit you could eat in her back yard. The backyard was a vineyard. She had bullet grapes, peaches, oranges, pears, figs, and tomatoes. She allowed us to eat our bellies full of whatever we wanted. Then early, early in the morning before the sun even came up she'd wake us up to a huge nutritious breakfast. The smell of her delicious crackling bacon was just divine. The smell of the bacon made you not even care about how early it was, we just enjoyed being away from home. Then on the ride home we'd crack jokes on each other the whole time.

Chapter 7 (When T.L. Came Back)

Upon arrival, there was a pleasant surprise. Not only had my mother rented us a home that was previously owned by my mothers brother. she was also pregnant with my little brother. The sad part was that she was pregnant from the same abusive man. He had come back to Daytona. It was probably around the year 1980 and my sister was only about three years old and my mom was now going to have two kids from him and the abuse continued. In spite of everything I loved the house, at first. It was a normal sized three bedroom house. The lawn was beautiful. It was fenced in and it sat on a hill. At the bottom of the hill and just around the bend was a grave yard. I started to think there was a ghost living with us, because crazy things used to go on. Things like rattling doorknobs and nobody there. Things like dog heads walking by the windows when the windows where to high for the head of a dog to be seen. One day during the middle of winter my little sister, brother and I were sleeping on the floor. The small bamboo wind chime that my mother had hanging from the ceiling started shaking vigorously. There was no wind because it was mid-winter and all the windows were closed and locked. My mother was at work at the time and when she returned, I told her what happened because we were very frightened, but she never believed me. I remember one night, my two cousins, two boys who were the same age as me, were staying over that night. All three of us heard the doorknob rattling as if there was someone trying to get in. We thought it was my older cousin, Poppa, trying to scare us. So we all dashed out the door at the same time to find that no one was there. We ran all around the outside of the house thinking he was hiding from us, but no one was there. Suddenly we became frightened and my cousin Red ran and locked himself in the linen closet and would not let us in. He stayed in there until my mother returned home. We were very shaken up, but again she did not believe us. All these crazy things would always happen when she was away. Therefore she never believed us. My attention was always divided between the ghost and T.L. Even though he cheated on her and beat her up all the time she loved him. It never mattered that she caught him cheating she was always the one to get beat up if she mentioned it. She went to a Christmas party sponsored by her job one year and he had told her not to go. She went anyway because she wanted to, and because he never let her go anywhere nor did he ever take her anywhere. When he came home and saw that she was not there, he went to the party and dragged her out. He took her to Tuscawilla Park and beat her mercilessly and he bit a plug out her buttocks. By the time he brought her home her clothes were torn, she could barely walk and she was filthy. She was beautiful when she left home. Then he comes in and tries to kiss her bottom where he had almost pulled a quarter sized plug out of her while begging her to forgive him and make love to him. I almost hated that man when I was growing up. When I was about nine years old he used give me and my cousins lit marijuana joints and tell us to hit it and we did. Then he would just laugh and laugh when we choked from the smoke. Even though my cousins were older than I was, all of us were under age. When my aunt found out that he gave it to her kids too she was furious. She came over and blasted him out and my mom to. Neither one of them ever did that again. Even After my mom had given this man 2 children he still continued to cheat on her and beat on her. I remember Every time my mother got herself a kitten he would take them far away, put them out of the car, and drive off so they couldn't come back, and when mom would ask him about them he would say they must have ran away. She was sad but she never knew, and he made me promise not to tell. The only good memory I have of T.L. was when he brought me a brand new beach cruiser. It was tall, blue, and had white walls on the tires. He put mirrors and chrome fenders on it. It was stolen from my cousin poppa after he begged me to let him ride it. I kept saying no but he just took it any way and I never saw the bike again. T. L. promised not to buy me another one if I let any one ride it, and he didn't. I remember One night my mother had a dream and I remember her saying how clear the dream was. She said she quickly got up and got dressed. She went to the place where had seen T.L. in her dream. When she got there she walked right up to the door and opened it. Everything was exactly as she had seen it in her dream. There was a white woman and a baby asleep on the sofa and T.L. was half naked asleep and uncovered in bed. She walked over to him and stuck her pistol against his nose which awakened him abruptly. He was petrified! He was explaining for dear life she said. By this time the woman was awake. She was crying scared too, but my mother simply said to him "I saw it all in my dream just as clear as the sky is blue. It's over. Please come and remove your things from my house immediately or they will be sitting along the roadside. And that was the end of him. My mother was deeply saddened and just hurt after that and became quiet and almost separated. Every day she would go to work, come home, cook or clean, take her shower and sit to the kitchen table working crossword puzzles while listening to the radio. That was her daily routine. She had stopped playing cards and watching T.V. with me and just kept to herself most of the time.

Chapter 8 (The Dark Tunnel)

I couldn't wait to get back to my aunt Lillie Mae's house where all my cousins were. That was the neighborhood. My uncle Bennie, my aunts husband used to cook my favorite dish which was smoked neck bones and rice. I liked it so much my uncle Bennie started calling me neckbone. He said I was so skinny that he was afraid to spank me cause I might break. So I always had the enjoyment of just watching my cousins get spanked. After dinner one night uncle Bennie told us to go to bed, but we just lowered our voices to a whisper and kept playing. When we thought my uncle and aunt were asleep we decided to get up and play a game that we made up called The Dark Tunnel. The house was a four bedroom two bathroom house with a long hallway. At night with all the lights off it's pitch black darkness. It was nine of us including my cousin Nikkei and myself and Poppa, Michelle, Karen, Daphne, Lynn, Red and Mann. We were all first cousins. We were the children of two sisters and one brother. In the game of the The Dark Tunnel Poppa would go hide in either one of the bedrooms or the bathroom and we each had to take turns at running down the hallway to try and reach the end without Poppa jumping out and scaring them half to death. We knew that if he caught you he was going to wrestle you to the ground and probably pinch you or bite you put you in some sort of a choke hold or whatever he may have seen on the wrestling channel earlier that day or something. Poppa was crazy but fun, you just never knew what to expect from him. By the time we got to the third or fourth person in our game of tunnel, we heard a voice say "yeah, come on down," It was my uncle Bennie. He was standing at the end of the hallway waiting. All we could see was the that white belt glowing in the dark. Everybody started crying. Nobody wanted to go first anymore. Even though nothing was going to happen to me, I was afraid for them. They got the spanking of their life while I kept count of every body's licks, then afterwards we'd just laugh at each other and how each one acted during their spankings. Karen was the worst of all. For some reason she could not just lay down and take her spanking like everyone else, she had to act a fool. Her spankings always lasted the longest because she would run, she would hide, she would do anything to resist it knowing that one way or the other it was going to happen. One time she ran and hid under the bed, which made it very difficult for my uncle to Bennie to spank her and every time he moved the bed, she would move with the bed. If he moved it all the way to the right side of the room, she moved with the bed and the same if he moved it left. This went on until he got down on his hands and knees and pulled her from under there, and she got it worse then. It seemed like child abuse at the time but kids really need that fear instilled in them or they go out and become menaces to society. Karen was the first one of us to start maturing into a young lady. The rest of us were jealous because Karen had a period before us and she had breasts before we did. We used to say "you don't have no titties, that's just fat." Karen was heavier than the rest of us so she would get angry when we'd said those mean things. Karen was also the first one of us to get pregnant, but throughout the entire pregnancy she kept saying that she never had sex before and she kept denying the pregnancy even when she was in labor. It was so funny, my aunt Lilllie Mae just laughed and laughed about that. Every time a labor pain hit Karen in the delivery room my aunt would say " you're a virgin ha?" and Karen would say "yes ma'am." And then my aunt would say " your never had sex before right?" and Karen would say "no ma'am." and my aunt would just laugh every time should told that story to one of friends or family members. Karen gave birth to a beautiful baby girl and named her Quanisha Mallory. But Karen wasn't the first to give birth, Lynn was. Even though Lynn was the youngest girl she was the first to have a baby. She named her son Darryl singleton Jr.

Chapter 9 (Losing my Virginity)

By the time I was fourteen some financial problems had forced my mom to move back in with my aunt Lillie Mae, and I was kind of happy about it cause It was fun in the creek. The real name of the neighborhood was Cedar Highlands but every body called it the creek. My best friend whom I met kindergarten lived out there, When I wasn't with my cousins, I would go around the corner to Michelle's house. Michelle and I had gotten to that age when teenagers start looking for trouble. We had another friend around the block name Francina. Francina had a brother named James that every girl in the creek wanted to be with, but James wanted me. Michelle and I both had boyfriends already but we were not having sex yet. We were still virgins. One day when I was walking alone and James walked up behind me. He had a football in his hand and he was just casually throwing it back and fourth from one hand to the other. He was also captain of the football team which was another reason why all the girls liked him. He walked up to me and said "hey girl; you are so pretty." I was smiling and I just thought I was on top of the world. But instead it was the worse thing that could have happened to any one. He asked me to come spend the night with him, and without thinking about it at all I did. I made up a lie right away to tell my mother. He said "I just love the way you walk!" And that just made me blush even more." Then he said, "do you want to be my girlfriend?" And I said, "yes." He said, "why don't you come over to my house and we can smoke some weed." He told me that he had a weed plant in his back yard that he had been growing and it was ready to be smoked. When we got there his mother was not at home. We went straight to his bedroom and we smoked the weed together. After we smoked a joint and then he started rubbing all over me and asking me to have sex with him. I was wearing a short shirt that stopped right above my navel and my shorts were very short also and that made it easy access. That was the day I lost my virginity. Some how, I thought he was going to love me forever but that was not his plan at all. I forgot all about my boyfriend who's name was name Tank. Then when I realized that James had other girlfriends and that he really did not care anything about me at all. In fact James had given me an STD the very first time that I had ever had sex. Then I in turn had given it Tank without even knowing that I had anything at all, because after James broke my virginity, then I broke Tank's virginity which caused and STD domino affect. Tank's mother took him to the doctor and then he came back and told me that I burnt him. Then I had to tell my mom what was going on because by then I was very irritated but was too young and dumb to even know that I was infected. It was gonorrhea. It was terrible to get an STD the very first time I ever had sex. My mother was furious, but after She took me to the doctor and I was cured. I never messed with James again and Tank never talked to me again. I was so embarrassed I didn't want to come out of the house for a long time. Later in life James had a car accident and was paralyzed from the waist down.

Chapter 10 (Another Abusive Man)

By 1983 my mother had me another man. His name was Robert Todd. He was a big man but not a fat man. He was very tall and had broad shoulders with a muscular build. He was very dark skinned and some what attractive. He talked in a smooth but finalizing toned voice. At first every body thought he was O.K. He had a nice car and we all liked it because it was pretty . It was a black Z28 and it was very fast. Every time he'd leave the house he'd sit in one spot and burn rubber before leaving. Just let the tires spin out. We all thought it was so funny, we would just laugh and laugh like no tomorrow. He and my mom dated for a while and she later became pregnant with her fourth child. All was well throughout the pregnancy and on April third she gave birth to my little brother who we called Teddy Bear as a nick name and Bear for short. The day she went in labor was Easter. As she stepped out the door carrying a platter of colored eggs that she planned to hide, her water broke. She had such a surprised look on her face, sort of like a deer caught in the headlights look, and she just stood there. Then realizing what had happened she yelled "my water broke! I'm in labor!" So they rushed her to the hospital and two hours later my brother bear was here. A few months later Robert began being abusive also to my mom and if I said anything about it, he would become verbally abusive to me. He didn't even care about doing it in my aunt's house. We were living with her when he started acting this way. Starting trouble was becoming a daily routine after work. Schlitz Malt Liquor Bull was the drink of the day for him. After drinking the third beer he would start mumbling to himself. You could never really hear what he was saying but he seem to get madder and madder the longer he mumbled. By the time he gets to the fourth, he was banging on the table. By the time he got to the fifth beer he was banging on my mom. At the entrance of the kitchen there were some nails hanging out from the top of the doorway and Robert had picked my mother up and was trying to ram her head upwards so that the nails would jam into her skull. When I realized what he was trying to do I ran as fast as I could and got a butchers knife and I was going to stab him in the back to save my mother but my uncle Bennie was just in time to snatch me up just before I could sink it into his back. Uncle Bennie saved his life cause I had had enough of men hurting my mother. I was to young at first but now I was old enough to help her to fight back, and I did. After that Robert hated me and I hated him too. I came in form school one day to find that he had cut the eyes out of my favorite school picture, and set it face down so that I would pick it up and see it. As soon as I saw it I knew he was the one who did it. I knew he was crazy but my mother let him talk her into moving into an apartment with him so I had to live with him too. Sure enough one day he came home with his beer and as usual, by the time he finished the fifth beer he started fighting my mom again. This time he was trying to drown her in the bath tub. I was so scared but I was not about to let him kill my mom. She was fully dressed and the bathtub was full of water and Robert had both his hands around her neck while she was on her knees and he was trying to force her body in the tub with the intent of drowning her when I walked into the bathroom. I jumped on his back and started punching him in the head, back and face. I was so afraid that he was going to be able to get my mom's head under that water because he was desperately trying to drown her. When he saw that I was not giving up, he let her go and he left. I told my mom right then and there that we were leaving. We gathered up what we could and we walked to me grandmother's house. I remember thanking God that Robert was out of our lives.

Chapter 11 (Meeting Draq)

So now we're living on the south side of Daytona instead of the west side. I had to change schools again and this time I was going to Seabreeze Junior high. I had to get used to ridicule all over again. Every morning and afternoon on the bus ride I had to hear silliness just because I was the new girl at the school. They talked about my skin, my hair, my clothes and anything else that they could think of. For some reason I was the target every day for this boy name Ervin who lived in Caroline Village, which is a housing complex.. He used to throw stuff at me when I got off the bus. Some days he might throw rocks or some days he may throw glass. He would say things like "I'm going to cut you too short to shit," for no apparent reason. He would just yell my name out and say rude and disrespectful things, and he didn't even know me. This nice guy named Herb had noticed all the terrible treatment I was getting and he offered to walk me home one day. Herb was very respectful and quite the gentleman. Herb was cute and he was tall. I liked him. When the fair came into town he asked if he could take me and I said yes. It was my first date and I was exited. At the fair Herb paid for everything I didn't need any money for anything. We played games together and shared cotton candy while watching the clown show. I really enjoyed that night. The next day after school he asked me to come with him to his house. Instead of getting off the bus at my bus stop I got off at his bus stop and then we walked to his house. He said that no one was there. Once inside we went straight to his bedroom. We started kissing and rubbing on each other and he started taking my clothes off. We got in the bed and under the covers. He didn't waist any time getting right in between my legs. Just as he entered about an inch of himself inside of me and we began the motion, his two little cousins walked in the room followed by his grandmother. We quickly grabbed our clothes and tried to get dressed as quickly as possible but they saw us naked. That was another embarrassing moment for me. Some years later Herb and one of his friends died in a car accident. They were simply waiting at the red light and some guys who were on a high speed chase running from the police crashed into their car and Herb and his friend were both killed instantly. It was a very sad time in our community. Herb and I had stopped seeing each other shortly after that embarrassing incident but he did have a child with another woman before he died. When I stopped seeing Herb I was just hanging out with a friend girl named Kim who I met at Seabreeze. Kim was pretty cool and she also lived in Caroline Village. She had a boyfriend named Darryl who had a nice pick-up truck. Darryl used to take us riding sometimes. Smoking weed and hanging out at Harlem Park became the thing to do. Until one day Kim said "lets go hangout with my cousin Tajuana today." Tajuana lived in Caroline village as Kim did but on the other end. So we walked down to Tajuana's house and Kim introduced us to each other and also to Tajuana's brother who had just come to live with her named Gerald. He told me that I could call him Gerry, but every body else called him Draq. He was a very attractive young man. He had a smooth dark complexion, medium height with a muscular build with a single gold tooth. He had nice, wavy, black hair with a sharp haircut. He was hot! And so was I. I had a banging body with an unusually small waist, perky breast and a perfectly round ass. Not to mention a face prettier than most. We hit it off immediately. I was crazy about him and he was crazy about me. He used to tell me how he loved to watch me walk. He said it was the most sexiest walk he'd ever seen. I started spending a lot of time over there and they'd have cookouts and parties and all Draq's friends used to come over and just crack on each other tell jokes and lies on one another and it was always fun and games. I first realized that he cared about me when I went to a party one night with Kim. It was a hot summer's night and all the girls were dressed really provocative. They were wearing either daisy dukes and halter tops or very mini, mini skirts. The party was in someone's backyard, and it was a huge backyard. Their was a D.J. set up and equipped with some very large speakers and there were a lot of teenagers there. It was a regular block party. Kim and I were having a good time and when the party was almost over, he came to pick me up. He had already told me earlier that he was going to pick me up after the party. For some reason, or another, I didn't believe him. Since he was older than I was, he was able to drive and I wasn't, and there were a lot of girls his own age who were crazy about him, and all these reasons made me believe he was surely going to dump me after he got what he wanted. But to my surprise, not only did he come to pick me up but he said very forcefully to his friend sitting in the front seat who thought he was going to continue to ride in the front seat, "Nigga get in the back, she's sitting in the front." And so he immediately his friend got in the back with his other 2 friends. After that his friends used to make fun and call him Donnie Knight the Ghetto Prince. That's when I knew he was starting to like me. Kim caught another ride home, So Draq just took all of his friends home and he and I went back to his room at his sister's house and that's where it all went down. That's when I was introduced to oral sex. I was 16 years old. I was aware of it and I had heard people talk about it before but I had never had the urge for it and basically I thought it was gross, until that night. Both of us had been drinking and smoking weed that night so we quickly aroused each other. He started kissing me everywhere and caressing me and undressing me all at the same time. He quickly undressed himself after undressing me and assisting me while motioning me to lie on the bed. Then he positioned himself on top of me and began kissing and sucking my breasts, while rubbing his hands on my thighs and easing his fingers right up between the wet lips of my vagina. I was truly enjoying the moment but then he seem to be moving downward, and then he starts kissing on my belly and then my navel. By then I started thinking to myself, is he going where I think he's going? I didn't really know what to do because I didn't want to seem any more immature than I already was. He was getting lower and lower, licking and sucking my bikini line and my hair line while squeezing and caressing my ass cheeks and thighs, and by now I'm really getting worried but I didn't want him to notice. I'm worried because I know I don't like the smell of vagina myself, so I'm worried about what's he going to think about it. But then he just put his face right in the middle of my private place and then I knew there really was such a thing as "eating pussy" because he was doing it to me. It was so sensual and sexual I seem to be making uncontrollable noises, that must've awakened his sister because the next day she was making fun of me. Tajuana had two little boys around the ages of two and three. The three year old was

Brian and the two year old was Broderick, but the boys couldn't pronounce each other's name properly so they called each other Bean and Brosco and so we all called them by the names they gave each other. The oldest boy named Brian took right to me. He used to say "that's my girlfriend" when he saw me coming. And every time that he was about to get a spanking he would yell out "spare the rod mommy! Spare the rod!" and we'd all just laugh and laugh. It was so funny to see him running around in just his underwear three years old and about three feet tall trying to keep from getting a spanking. Tajuana would be laughing so hard that she couldn't spank him. Then the next time I came over he taught me how to give him oral sex. First he told me to kiss his penis, which I did. Then I started licking it, and not wanting to seem immature, I started stroking it and jacking it. He seemed to enjoy it cause then he told me to suck it. So I was just sucking the head part for a while and he said "you're supposed to put the whole thing in your mouth." I tried it but I felt like I was choking and I thought I was going to throw up. Once I got the hang of it and was able to relax more, I got better and we were doing it all the time to each other. I told Draq that I was a little self conscious about my smell and he said "I like your smell, in fact your new name is sweet sixteen, cause you smell sweet and your sixteen years old." Then I didn't feel so crazy. We were having a very nice relationship when one day he just up and said "my mom said I have to move back to Miami." He had been living there before he came here with his sister, and his mom wanted him to come back home. When he left I didn't see him for a long, long, time, so I just moved on.

Chapter 12 (Meeting my Sister for the First Time)

I was still going to school at that time but I was being retained for skipping too much. I always made straight A's when I was there but the absences caused me to fall behind in my grades, so I just decided to drop out of school in the ninth grade because I refused to repeat it. I was some what of a rebellious kid and my mother never really yelled at me or anything and my dad wasn't in my life cause he chose another family to raise, therefore I pretty much did what I wanted to do. I remember when my daddy introduced me to my sister that I didn't even know I had. She also was from a woman that he just walked away from after he got her pregnant. He took us on a shopping trip together at Montgomery Ward. Her name is Tina and she was a few years younger than me. I never thought to ask my dad why we were just meeting each other but I was happy that we were all together. My dad has six children but he only raised the last three because he married their mother. The three of us were bastard children from three separate woman who were left to raise us the best way that they could. I always honored him even though I often wondered what my life would have been like had he raised me. I wondered what was wrong with my mom, and why couldn't he have married her? I was his first born child. My mother's mother told me that we were to poor for his parents. My mother came from the projects and his family were well established school teachers so that meant that he was to good for her. So his mother moved him to Bell glades, Fl to keep them apart but he went and made another child there. I wonder if my other two outside siblings have the same emotions I have. Either way God made a way for all of us to survive with or without our father. He made sure all of his kids had college educations except me. That has always bothered me but I never said a word. Most of the time I try to think about good times I had with him. Like one time I spent the night at my grandmother's house and my three cousins from his side of the family were there and we played and had so much fun that we were up all night. I remember my dad yelling upstairs for us to quiet down because were so loud. The next morning, very early before the sun was completely up, I felt something moving in my nose. I thought I was dreaming at first. It felt like maybe the covers were moving back and fourth from the wind of the fan but when I opened my eyes there was a huge palmetto bug right on the tip of my nose. I screamed so loud that I woke up the whole house and everybody thought that was so funny. I guess they were used to the palmetto bugs but I was not. I never spent the night over there again.

Chapter 13 (When Crack Came Out)

After dropping out of school, I started hanging out with another girl I knew from school named Carol. She was younger than me but she seemed a lot older at times. She was living in a rooming house with her man and I do mean man because he was about thirty when she was only fifteen. His name was Curt. He was a drug dealer and had large amounts of drugs in the room at all times. We could have been arrested or robbed or worse, but we were too young to realize potential danger. Carol and I spent a lot of time in the room because he never allowed her to go anywhere. She was a very attractive young lady and he was jealous and over protective of her because she kept herself up nicely. She always kept her hair done and wore nice clothes and she was very light skinned. He gave her money and weed to smoke everyday but she couldn't leave the room. Our other home girl Vanessa would come over some time and we would have singing contest on the tape recorder just to past time and keep us occupied. That's when I realized that I had a nice singing voice. When Curt had left the room one day Carol showed us the drugs he was selling and she said you can smoke this but only when it's in weed. Never smoke this by itself. It will make you unable to stop. She said the name of this is crack rock. To me it looked like a big flat cookie. Carol said girl, that's just what this much of it is called, a cookie. This drug was sweeping the nation. It was the first time I had ever heard about it. Carol told me that this drug was very potent and you will get addicted to it and fast. All you have to do is hit it once by itself and you would be hooked. So we were very careful to only smoke it in weed. We would place the piece of rock in a piece of paper, fold the paper together and crush the rock up real fine until it reaches powder form and lace it in a marijuana joint and smoke it. We called them juice joints Or geek joints. We didn't realize it was addictive that way too just at a much slower and less aggressive rate. Smoking it straight by itself just took you quickly to rock bottom. So many lives were being ruined from this drug which resulted in so many families being torn apart. I came home from Carol's house one day and right afterwards my Uncle Robert knocked on the door. He rushed in talking loud telling my mom " look what I got," as if it was something good. He said, "you ain't never seen no shit like this peewee, you're going to love it." He had a big, round, glass bowl with a stem on each end, allowing two people to smoke crack from it at the same time. "This is the ultimate high right here peewee," he said. That's when I knew it was crack. I said, "no! Mama wait, you can't smoke this stuff alone you have to smoke It in weed. " I said , "I'll be right back I'm going to get you some weed and do not smoke until I get back." I left but when I returned she had already smoked it and he was showing her how to (bring it back.) That's when they pour a small amount of clear alcohol into whatever they were smoking out of, in this case a bowl, and swish it around making sure to coat the entire inside of the bowl and then pour the residue filled alcohol from the bowl onto a piece of glass such as a mirror and set it on fire. Once the fire has burned out and the substance on the mirror has dried, which only a few minutes, then they scrape it of using a razorblade and simply place it back in the bowl and smoke it again. This whole process is called bringing it back, or smoking the backwash. From that day forward my mother just continuously wanted more and was unsuccessful at living a normal life. My Uncle just kept coming around feeding her more and more everyday. I kept asking her not to smoke it like that but she wouldn't listen. I was still geeking myself so I couldn't really stop her so from doing anything so I

just went back out in the creek to my aunt Lillie Mae's house. Me and Daphne were chillin with our friend Gertrude who lived down the street. We had been smoking but we had run out of crack and between the three of us all we had left was ten dollars. We wanted some more crack but we didn't have a car but Jake did. Jake was Gertrude's boyfriend so Gertrude had to sneak Jakes car while he was asleep and it was well after midnight. We managed to steal the car and off we went. We really didn't know where to get it from so we were just riding and looking. Then we saw a man walking down rose street . He was walking with a cane, so we didn't think he would be out selling crack but he was. He said, "hey, what do you all want?" I said who are you? He said "I'm Ray King." We just looked at each other at first cause we were surprised to see and older man with a cane this late at night selling crack, but we gave him the money any way and he gave us the crack. Anxiously we rushed home and we got ready to crush it up and realized it wasn't crack at all. I don't know what it was but we were pissed off. There was nothing we could do. After that Daphne never smoked any more. I just start smoking with my friend Michelle from around the corner. One day Michelle and I were just chillin, walking around looking for something to get into, and we ran into these two guys from the neighborhood and they were just walking too. We knew them, and they were looking for something to get into also. They told us that they had some crack and that we could come smoke with them if we wanted to. We all walked around the corner to this empty house were the people had just got evicted and we knew the people and we knew that were gone so we thought it would be a good place to go chill. As we're walking up the driveway we heard an old lady yell from her window, "that's trespassing, don't go in there."" Don't you all see that sign?" But we just waved our hands at the old lady and went inside anyway. The guys had made these little home made smoking pipes out of milk jug handles and named them uzzies. They cut the handle off of the plastic milk jug from the top to the bottom taking only the handle from the jug and wrapped some foil around the wide end of the handle and poked holes in the middle of the foil and place cigarette ashes on top, then the crack rock on top of the ashes and put fire to it and inhale. Just as soon as we started smoking off the uzzie, knowing I had been for warned about smoking straight crack, I did it any way. As soon as I took my first hit, The police pulled into the driveway. Everybody started running. I tried to jump out of a back window but when I jumped out of the window my foot got caught and I fell on my knee and the officer was right there. I didn't even have time to stand up. They took us all to jail, but they let us go on R.O.R.. Everybody except Michelle cause there was a warrant out for her arrest for driving without a license. I think she had to stay for thirty days. When she did get out we started hanging out in the bottom.

Chapter 14 (The Bottom)

The bottom was a group of clubs next door and across the street from each other. they were all located at the end of a street called Martin Luther King Jr. Blvd., at the south end of town. I guess that's why the named it the bottom cause it was at the end the street at the end of town. It was three clubs, one was called the Trop, one was called Fuller's and the other was Georges Place. The bottom was so much fun we would walk from any where to get there. You could play pool in any one of the clubs in the bottom. There was a Dance Hall and mixed drinks in Georges Place and at the Trop you could get beer and Ms. Edda's delicious fried chicken sandwich, spicy pork chop sandwich or one of her huge and juicy cheese burgers. All ms. Edda's food was good after a long night of dancing and getting high and drinking. It was packed with people no matter which night you went in the bottom. That's when the bottom was the most fun, but sometimes trouble would find it's way and people were sometimes hurt really bad or even killed. A friend of mine named Kay Kay, was an innocent by stander when she was gunned down. She was just in the wrong place at the wrong time. She was standing outside in front of Georges Place and a stray bullet fired from inside struck her in the head, and she was killed instantly. It was so sad, just a never forgotten senseless tragedy. Another senseless tragedy was about a young man who one night he and his brother robbed some other boys while chillin in the bottom. They pointed guns at them and took their stuff. They called them all kinds of names and then sped away. The next night these same two robbers where in the bottom again and the boys they robbed the night before came back and retaliated. One of the brothers ran and left the other and those boys beat him unmercifully. I mean they beat him, they kicked him, they stomped him to sleep. They left him there shaking violently from the convulsions and he almost died. He lay there helplessly until the ambulance finally arrived. The next time I saw that boy, maybe two or three months later, he was in a wheelchair and he was paralyzed from the waist down. Ignoring the danger we continued to go to the bottom. Most of the time we were smoking geek joints in the bathrooms or just drinking and dancing in the clubs. One night we were in the men's bathroom in the Trop smoking crack. It was me, Michelle, another girl named Loleeta and a girl named Neicy. All of a sudden the door swung open and It was a big black man named Johnny heart. Every body knew him but we didn't know what he came to do. When he walked in he had a gun in his hand that looked just like the one I had seen as a child. It was a thirty eight special. It had a long silver barrel, and a pearl white handle. He said, "bitch I told you I was going to find you didn't I?" He was talking to Loleeta. I don't know if she stole something from him or not but he was pissed off. Every body else ran except Loleeta and me, I was to busy trying to gather my rocks off the counter and she was to scared to move. I gathered my rocks quickly and I ran too. We were all standing outside in front of the club scared to death for her but waiting to see what was going to happen. Somebody had already called the police but by the time they got there he was gone and nobody dared to stop him cause he was a known woman beater and a man beater. When she came out of that bathroom her once white dress was completely red from her own blood. Her hair was soaked with blood and it had ran all down her legs and onto her shoes. She was literally bloody from head to toe. He had pistol whipped her real bad. The ambulance came and they took her to the hospital and after a while she was back to her old self again. Being a teenager you don't realize the potential dangers that leark in the night. I've walked through wooded on dirt roads alone before while holding a retractable blade in my hand. I walked through these areas in the midnight hours before, just to get to the bottom. It wasn't uncommon to walk cause that was the only place teenagers could hang out without having to show I.D.

Chapter 15 (Being Abused Myself)

One night while walking alone down cypress street, on my way to the bottom, a guy on a motorcycle just pulls right along side of me and takes off his helmet and says to me, "I think you have the most sexiest walk I've ever seen on a woman and what is your name." I told my name and he told me his name. It was Charles. He wasn't very attractive but he offered me a ride and a compliment so I accepted. He gave me his helmet cause he only had one and off we went. He road me around for a while and I enjoyed it. I had never been on a motorcycle before but I like it so I continued to ride with him and then he took me to get me some thing to eat and we went back to his room. I think it was a rooming house but I'm not sure. I just know it was were he lived. He asked me to stay the night with him but I said no because I knew he wanted to have sex with me and at that time I was on my period so I told him no. He said, "I don't care nothing about that." I thought he meant he just wanted me to stay without having any sex, but no, he said, "we can still have sex I don't care about the blood." I said "are you crazy?" I had never heard of anything like that. He said "there's nothing wrong with doing that, people do it all the time. Even though I felt strange and stupid, I let him do it anyway. But before we had intercourse, he gave me oral sex knowing that my menstrual cycle was on and then he said, you're in my system now. After that he would not let me out of his sight. Over a short period of time he became very controlling and even abusive and I had never even said that I was his girlfriend. He locked me in a room in his mothers house one day and he wouldn't let me out nor would he let his mother or brothers in. He was holding a motorcycle pipe to my face and threatening to hit me with it if I tried to get out. He told me that I wasn't going any where until he said so. His mom was screaming at him from the other side of the door and He was screaming at me and I was screaming just cause I wanted to get out of there and I was scared to death. I didn't know what this fool had in mind for me. Hours later after he finally calmed down, he decided he was going to go to the motorcycle races that night. I was glad cause I knew this was my chance to get away. When he left, I left. I was walking as fast I could trying to get home before he saw me. Then out of all the people in the world to run into, I ran into Draq. He was back . I was so happy to see him and he was happy to see me. I didn't go home right then I went with Draq. He was like my knight in shining armor coming to take me away. It was a wonderful coincidence that at that precise time we ran into each other again after all that time. It must have been close to a year since I had seen him. We went back to his sisters house and we made passionate love that night. It was so amazingly beautiful after all that time away from each other. I told him that I had another friend but I did not want to be with him any longer and that I was in the process of leaving when I saw him and that's why I was walking so fast. So after our rendezvous Draq's walking me home and we're holding hands and I look up and see Charles at the red light. He was in his car instead of his motorcycle and he looks over and see's me. When the light changed for him to go, he slowly cruised under the light, I guess to make sure that it was me, and then in a loud and stern voice he said "Trece! Come here!" I was so scared. I told Draq to go, that I would call him the next day. Draq said "are you sure?" "yes" I said," go!" So he left. Then Charles parked his car on the curbside of the road and got out and walked across the street to me and took one hand and put it around my neck and lifted me up off of the ground and walked me back to his car just like that. My feet never touched the ground at all from one side of the street to the other side of the street. When he got me to his car he slammed my head into the top of his car. Immediately I could feel a huge knot forming on my forehead. The pain was so great that I literally saw stars. It was total darkness and a million stars. I was so dizzy, I didn't know where I was. Then he tried to force me into his car from the driver side, but I would not get in because at the same time he was trying to force me in the car he was telling me that that he was going to kill me. So somehow I tore away from him and I ran to the other side of the car but he chased me so I just kept running around and around the car until he just jumped over the top of the car and grabbed me. This time he was telling me things like I'm going to take you to Deland and kill you and leave your body in a ditch alongside the road. He said, "you think that was something when I took my baby's mama to the grave yard at midnight and kicked that bitch out of my car in the middle of the graveyard? Bitch that ain't nothing compared to what I'm going to do to you." He was choking me at the same time and tying to get me into the passenger side of his car. He had me almost inside too but I stretched my leg over to the horn and I laid my foot on the horn. I kept my foot on that horn for as long as I could cause I wanted some body to see what he was doing to me and help me. I guess Draq heard the horn and he came back. Charles was choking me so hard that I thought I was about to pass out at any moment. Then just at the nick of time Draq said, "let her go man." But no response from Charles, I mean he was choking me good and again Draq said "man let her go!" still no response, that third time Draq said "man I'm not going to tell you again to let her go!" Then suddenly Draq hit Charles so hard and fast and repeatedly that he fell to the ground where Draq continued to punch him until I yelled, "Draq lets go!" When Draq got up I could see that Charles's entire face was covered in blood. We started running. I could see Charles going into his trunk and I told Draq that he was getting a stick. There was a stick that he always kept in the trunk that he said was just in case he was loosing, and he had definitely lost that fight. I thought he was going to hit Draq with the stick but he was strictly after me. He wanted to kill my in any way that he could. I was running for my life. My house was only about a block away. As I was running I looked back to see where he was and he was right behind me Draq was across the street trying to pull a century 21 sign up out of the ground. Just as I got to the corner of my street, Charles caught me. I was in a neighbors front yard when he grabbed both my arms and twisted them around and around each other and with one swift yank, he flipped my whole body over and I fell on some bowling ball sized rocks that were in the neighbors front yard. I fell flat on my back on top of the rocks. Then out of no where Draq hit him in his back with that century 21 sign. He fell on the ground and I started running again. I made it to my house and I was banging on the back door and yelling for my mother. She was asleep because was it was very late. I looked behind me to see where he was and he was almost to me so I took off running around the side of the house to the front door and I started banging as hard as I could and just as he was about to get to me my mother opened the door and I ran. Then he ran in behind me and then Draq ran in behind him. Every body was talking at one time trying to explain to my mom what was going on. Charles was covered in blood and dripping it everywhere so my mom hands him one of our hand towels to clean himself up. I said "ma, don't give him our towel he just tried to kill me." My mom just told them both to leave and the next day Charles came back to beg me to stay with him. His eyes were swollen shut almost and his nose and lips were black and blue and they were busted open. He looked like a monster. I never spoke to him again. Later I heard he was sent to prison for 10 years for beating up another lady.

Chapter 16 (Being Hard Headed)

When I saw Draq again I was so thankful that he had saved my life that night, because I could've been killed by that fool. But that didn't stop me from hanging out and smoking cigarettes, drinking beer, smoking weed or geeking. I just kept right on partying. Not listening to my mother and just carrying on as if I was grown. The old people called it being fast. I remember my mom told me to stay home one day; "do not leave this house today" she said. But I disobeyed her of course and went to Caroline village. It was always live in the village in the evenings after the hottest part of the day had passed. A whole gang of people used to hang out. There were teenagers everywhere and I was standing in the middle of a crowd that was posted up in the middle of the street. When all of a sudden a car pulled up and it was my mom. She was in the car with her new boyfriend Sam. He was driving while she scanned the neighborhood's looking for me. She had never done this before so I didn't realize how angry she was. They pulled right up along side the crowd and my mother said, in a very serious but low tone "get in this car or I will beat you down right where you stand." Well to save myself any embarrassment, I quickly got into the car. She had a look in her eyes that I had never seen before. When I got in the car all she said was "didn't I tell you not to leave that house today?" I said , in very sorrow filled voice "yes." Then she said , "O.K.", and the rest of the ride home was extremely silent, even Sam seemed scared to talk. As soon as we got inside the house she pushed me really hard into the refrigerator and started punching me and shoving me and slapping me. It was as if she was fighting another woman in the streets. The whole time while she was beating me down she kept saying, "you want to act like you're grown, I'm going to beat you like you're grown. This is a grown woman beat down right here!" It was to shocking to me. This behavior was totally out of character for her, but I guess I had really pissed her off. After all that had happened it still didn't stop me. She told me to go to my room and stay. I was on punishment and only allowed to come out to eat. Now I'm laying down in my room thinking about what had just happened, when I hear a voice at my window. It was my cousin Red. He was there when my mother came and took me away. So now he's at the window and he's telling me to lets go. He said "who the hell does Aunt Peewee think she is, shit you're seventeen years old, she should not be still trying to hit you. Let's go!" he said., and he began to take the screen out of the window. I said, "Shhhhhhhh!" I was trying to listen to make sure she wasn't coming. So carefully and ever so quietly, I climbed out of the window and jumped on the handlebars of the Red's bicycle and we rode off. I left with only the clothes on my back. Not once did I even think about where I was going to lay my head that night or the next, or where my next meal was coming from. I had no money and no job so I was real stupid for leaving like that. We went riding around to all of our little hangout spots with me on the handlebars. Later, we ended up back in Caroline Village cause there was a party going on in the middle of the field. I mingled and partied all night and when the party was over I didn't have a ride, nor did I have any where to go. I was afraid to go home and at that time I was unaware of the fact that my mom had told my sister and brothers not to let me in if I came there. There was a young man at the party and as everyone else was leaving he said he noticed that I didn't have a ride. He told me that his name is Blue and he offered me a ride, but I told him I couldn't go home. Once I explained my situation to him then he offered to get me a room. I quickly accepted and jumped into his truck. He had two pickup looking trucks but they had no beds on them they were just the cab part of the truck with some wooden slabs that attached the tires to the truck. He told me that he also had a car and a motorcycle. He told me that his real name was Bernard Washington and he was currently studying to be an auto body mechanic. He was attending D.B.C.C., the local community college, and he had just received his student loan check. We had been talking for hours before we realized that we lived on the same street only two house down from each other. That was strange that we had not seen each other before. He seemed to be a good guy at the time. He was very polite and courteous and he was about four years older than me. We seemed to hit off right away. He paid for us to stay in that hotel room for about two weeks and he bought me some clothes and food. When the money ran out we simply went to his house and stayed there. I was nervous about staying at his house cause it was so close to my house. After a few days there I needed more clothes so I decided to walk up the street behind our house to see if maybe I would see one of my siblings so I would know if my mom was home or not. Well I guess they saw me before I saw them and yelled to mama, "Trece is outside on the back street." But I didn't hear them tell her cause they were inside but before I knew anything she was right in my face. I was so nervous , I didn't know what she was going to do., but she just stared at me and said "so this is what you want Trece Ann? You want me to just let go and watch you walk away ha?" And I said, "yes." We both turned and walked away from each other. I know that hurt my mom cause it hurt me and I really don't know to this day why I said that to my mom cause she was a good mom. I didn't realize at the time how bad I hurt her when I said that awful and inconsiderate word to my mother. It often haunts me to know that I said such painful things to my once beautiful and loving mother. Later in my mature years I asked god for forgiveness for my ignorance which I believe to this day caused my mom to completely surrender herself to crack. I feel that It is my fault, so I keep the faith that one day God will give her back to us clean and sober with a heart filled with love as she was before. I have since learned to honor my mother as God has commanded.

Chapter 17 (Becoming a Mother)

I continued to chill with Bernard. We had some good times, like riding around on his motorcycle all bundled up from the cold. We'd have socks on our hands and scarfs on our faces and necks while riding wild in the cold. It used to a lot of fun. Some time afterwards, maybe a few months, I realized I was pregnant. I was scared and I didn't want to tell my mom for fear that she would try to talk me into getting and abortion. I was afraid that if I got an abortion, God would be so displeased with me that he may not bless me with another child and I didn't want to take that chance. I didn't tell anyone until it was too late for me to get an abortion. My grandmother Rosa B. Tiller had taught me very well what the Lord God had expected of us and It was not to kill. It was a blessing from God and I didn't want to loose my chance of ever having a child. I knew very well what was unacceptable in his eyes. One of my grandmothers favorite sayings was "Don't take what you can't give back," which means If you can't breath life back into that baby's body then don't take life out of her body. I understood very well. Even if it was only a spider or a grasshopper thou shall not kill. When I finally told my mom it was past my time so I could keep the baby. My mother was mad but she didn't act all crazy like I thought she was going to act. I guess by then she was pretty far gone on crack because I don't think she really thought about it. Ever since I had told her to let me go , she had been smoking straight crack full force every day. She was to far gone. Thank God my pregnancy was normal, I didn't have any complications at all. At first Bernard was there, then later in the pregnancy he got lost. My cousin Karen had her own apartment at that time in Soul City and Daphne was also pregnant but she was about four months farther than I was. One night Bernard was there with all of us at Karen's house. Daphne was there Karen and her boyfriend and her daughter Kee Kee who was about three years old. Karen had a one bedroom apartment with a pull out sofa in the living room which is where I slept. I was living with Karen at that time because my mother and her boyfriend Sam had moved into another house down on Seagrave St. I tried to stay there but the first night I stayed there I could hear huge rats walking around on the wooden floor. The house looked like It was built in the 1800's. It was a very old house and it was big. It had tall ceilings an attic and a huge pyramid shaped roof with the point at the top. I could hear the rats clearly and inside the house. It was so dark that you couldn't see anything except pitch black. There was only one street light on the whole street and it was halfway up the street. The rats sounded heavy, you could hear them jump form the cabinets to the stove and from the stove to the floor. You could hear anyone walking on the floor because the house and floor was wooden. So I'm laying there scared to move. Plus I'm about five or six months pregnant, so I was heavier. I know somehow I had to feel around in the dark for my shoes because the electricity had not been turned on yet. So I felt around in the dark and finally I felt my shoes and put them on quietly, stepping ever so lightly trying not to step on any rats. In the dark and pregnant I walked to my cousin Karen's house and she allowed me to stay with her. That's why we were all at Karen's hose, the only time during the pregnancy that he spent the night with me. We had fun that night though because we were up all night. Bernard just kept me and Daphne in tears all night, laughing at him, and then the next morning is when I found out that Bernard had just had a baby from another female who lived just down the sidewalk from Karen. She lived in the same complex. When he was leaving the next morning, I saw him talking to her on the corner. She had a baby stroller with his baby in it. I felt so stupid. After that I didn't see him any more until two weeks after my baby was born. All my cousins had already had one child and Daphne had two by the time I had one. It was the baby boom for our family. After I had lived with my cousin Karen a couple months, her boyfriend named Versa Lee, told her he wanted privacy and that she needed to kick me out and she did. At 8 months pregnant my cousin Karen kicked me out for a man who was just using her apartment for somewhere for himself to stay cause he didn't have anywhere to go himself. So then I went to live with my other Aunt, named Eva Lee. I had said that I wasn't going to have anymore kids because of all the pain and discomfort throughout the whole pregnancy and then the tremendous amount of pain to give birth. Even worse for me was when I went into labor early that morning, probably about 7:30 a.m. I thought my stomach was hurting because I had held my urine too long. When I went to the rest room I noticed blood and I told my aunt and she said I was going into labor. So now I'm alarmed and I went to find my mother. After so many months had passed and my mother was smoking crack so much more that by then her and Sam had lost the house and broken up and she was staying with some lady named Betty on Walker Street. We rode around for at least two hours looking for my mom so that she could go with me to the hospital. When we found her she didn't want to come but I told her if she didn't come I would have the baby there. Then she finally came with us. It was me, my mom, my cousin Michelle, and my cousin Karen. I stayed in labor at least fourteen hours. I did not give birth until 10:58 p.m from &:30 a.m. I guess at about 6 p.m. my mom began getting impatient, and she said she was leaving. I was in a great deal of pain and I told her that if she left I would pull these monitors and IV off me and follow her if she tried to leave me. She was so ready to smoke that she was no longer willing to see her grandchild be born. My cousin Michelle then took it upon herself to talk to my mother and make her stay. Immediately after my baby girl was born, my mother left. I was not mad at her, I just thanked God for letting her be there for the time that she was. It was a blessing in itself. I named my baby Jo'Quala Reve' Worsham. When we were released from the hospital my baby and I went to live with my Aunt Eva Lee. She lived around the corner from my other Aunt. Both lived in the creek. My Aunt Eva Lee was a foster mother so there were always different kids living with her. Some were white some were mixed and others were black. She gave me a place to stay and I was very grateful. I stayed there for a while. After I was strong enough I went in search for a job. I got hired pretty quickly at Wendy's. It was my first job and I was happy to have it. It was a struggle sometimes trying to catch the votran to take Quala to the doctors and for me to get to work. We had no transportation and I remember standing out in the cold trying to shelter myself and my baby from the wind while waiting for the bus to come. But I did whatever I had to do to maintain with no help from Bernard. My aunt would help keep Quala for me while I worked, but for days like going to the wic office, the store for milk and pampers, and doctor appointments for me and the baby, I was on my own to get there. My only transportation was the votran. It was hard at first but I was very strong-minded, but for some reason I went back to stay with my mom.

Chapter 18 (Rock Bottom)

Some how she had gotten another apartment and I was back home and I was glad. At first things seemed o.k. but then my mom started smoking real heavy again. At first I was just geeking and then one day when I couldn't find any weed. My mama said, "girl you better hit this stem like me and Thelma." Thelma was my mom's next door neighbor and I had never smoked from the stem before. The stem was a glass pipe that had a small amount of brillo stuffed in one end of it. You put the rock in the end where the brillo is, stick a flame to it and smoke. The brillo acts as a filter on a cigarette . To smoke in this manner, off a stem, was the quickest way to get addicted to crack. When she said that, I knew that if I didn't hit it like that I just wouldn't get any at all. So of course I hit it. That was my ultimate downfall. I started smoking off the stem. Like mother, like daughter. From that day, I started doing all kinds of things for crack. I was spending more time with the next door neighbor named Thelma who was also a baser. She was very devious. She was a known thief and she used a girdle to steal out of stores. She would put on a long and wide dress, then pull a girdle up to her thighs and then simply put whatever she wanted in the girdle and pull the dress back down to cover it. She did this a lot to support her crack habit. One late night after running our of crack we wanted some more. So she said, " come on girl, I know just what to do." We left walking, and Thelma was very persuasive, she could talk her way out of anything. When we got to the corner she hollered us a ride down, cause anybody going up MLK Blvd. we knew they were going to the bottom. So we get down to the bottom and the person who gave us a ride said they would bring us right back home too. Soon as Thelma see a dealer, she flags him over to the car and asked for a twenty dollar rock and as soon as he hands it to her she hands him a one dollar bill all balled up so that he couldn't see what it was. Then in an urgent voice she yells to the driver "go! Go!" He drives off and I see the man looking at the money and then he put his hand in his pocket, and I knew he was reaching for a gun. Thelma was screaming, "drive faster, drive faster!" I was so scared but Thelma would do stuff like this all the time without letting me know what she was about to do. Then one day, probably the next day, she and I went across the river to search for a job. Actually I think we were just looking for a way to steal. The first application we put in was a maid position. The lady hired us both on the spot. She said she was desperate and had much work for us to do. She gave us keys to the rooms and carts full of supplies to clean the rooms with. We were cleaning really good at first but then Thelma found some money in her second room. She took two hundred dollars and left the rest. She came running up to the room where I was working and showed me the money. She said, " I got two hundred dollars, one for me and one for you but there's a lot more down there." I said, "why didn't you get all of it you dummy?" She said, "I don't know I got scared." So I said, "lets go back." We scanned the area to see if any one was watching, then we made a dash for the room were the money was. We unlocked the door with the key and went in and got the money. As we were leaving we noticed some one coming in through the back door and we could see their silhouette through the glass on the door. So we snatched the money and ran. We paid a man at the fish market one hundred dollars to take us back across the river to home. In all we had nineteen hundred dollars and they were all one hundred dollar bills. We smoked all that money up with out paying any bills and without having any thing to show for it. Then my mother stopped paying the bills again. First the water got turned off. We couldn't bathe. Then the lights got turned off and we had no food, and no way of keep my baby's bottles cold. That caused maggots to form in her bottles from the heat and I didn't know it. By this time Bernard had a new girlfriend and they wanted to keep Quala for a while to help me out because they knew my situation. Then he came and got her and took her back to his place. He told me that the milk would not come out of the bottle while he was trying to feed her so he took the top off the bottle and there were maggots in the bottle and the milk was clumped up and smelled spoiled. He came and found me and slapped my face so hard I didn't know what happened. He said, "bitch what the fuck's wrong with you? Why the fuck are there maggots in my baby's bottle?" I explained to him that my mother didn't pay the electric bill and I had nowhere to keep her bottles. He had never seemed to care before but this really angered him. I was so busy smoking crack that I didn't even know there were maggots in the bottles. I felt really bad after that but not bad enough to stop smoking. So he and his girlfriend kept my baby for me for about a week or two. It was 1987 and During that time was when my mother simply walked away one day and she never came back home . All I know is that one day the landlord came and put all our stuff outside on the trash pile.

He put a huge pad on our door and an eviction notice. I'm unsure of how long it had been sense she had paid the rent but they didn't give us any chance to get our things. There was no warning to my knowledge at all. When they came I was there with my brother T.J. My brother Bear and my sister Tammie had spent the night with her friend Heather and my mom never went back to get her so the lady raised her and thank God for that white woman with a big heart who took it upon herself to take care of my sister without any assistance from either of her parents. When they put our stuff out and locked the doors I had no choice but to get to walking. I walked my brother T.J. to my grandmother's house and asked her to call his dad, but she didn't, she called my Aunt Lille Mae and she came and got T.J and kept him until his dad was able to come get him and he kept hem and raised him. Then I took my brother Bear to his grandmother on his fathers side and she raised him until he later went to prison. So that left me walking the streets with no where to go. First, I went back to the garbage pile with all our stuff on it and I found my only pair of sneakers. They were a black pair of high top Reeboks. That's all I took from our belongings that were now a pile of garbage. I felt so alone at that moment in my life. I can still remember what I was wearing that day. I had on a blue topless one piece jumpsuit that had Hawaiian flowers all over it. I remember it so clearly because it was one of my favorites. I walked and walked the lonely streets and then I met a man. He was a baser too, and homeless just like me. He introduced himself to me as Pretty Slim. He said his real name was Johnny Carol. I thought the name sounded like a stage name for a movie star or some rock star maybe. He was very tall with a slender build and a dark complexion. He was what I call a professional thief. I called him that cause he could steal the sweet out of sugar. He made a living out of stealing. I guess you can say that after that day we were partners in crime. He went and stole some food for us to eat and later he went to the mall and stole some dresses, and then sold them. That's how we were able to get a hotel room for the week. This went on for days. Every day he would steal something and sell it in order for us to survive. He didn't even know me very well and he was risking his freedom to take care of me. He would wear a stomach girdle under a very loose fitting shirt and what ever he wanted he simply stuck it under his shirt in between the girdle and his skin. The girdle would hold everything in place for him so it was easy. All he had to do was move fast enough while I kept the clerk or clerks occupied. It was an elaborate scheme that worked every time. I know it was wrong but I was on crack. Slim used to like for me to perform oral sex on him while he was hitting the pipe. It was his favorite way to get off. That's what I had to do in turn for him supplying my every need. One day Slim left on his daily routine while I stayed in the room. when he came back he had two white guys with him. He was trying to juggle them out of their money somehow. He was going to let them sit at the room with me while he went to get them crack. The white boys decided one would go with him and the other would stay with me. I guess they didn't really trust him that much. Slim and one of the guys left while the other guy and myself stayed at the room. While they were gone he introduced himself to me as Mark and I said, " hi, my name is Trece. " At first it was just small talk. Then just out of the blue with a pleading look on his face he said "I got some money in my pocket, do you think you could probably let me have a little shot of ass?" I was shocked. I had never had sex with a white person before. In fact I remember saying that I would never have sex with a white person before but again, I was on crack and he had such a sincere look in his eyes, that I said "yes." He quickly gave me the money and jumped right in bed with me. I was already sitting on the bed and he was sitting on the other bed at first. We both hurried to take our clothes off cause I didn't know how soon Slim would be back, and we got under the covers together. He quickly got between my legs and he was hard immediately and he entered me immediately. Then immediately it was over. I called it a quickie because it did not last long before he was done. It was probably about ten minutes at the most. After that he was hooked. He had already given me money. Then he just stayed there and kept buying crack for us all to smoke and then when he got ready to leave he asked me to go with him, but it wasn't until after he had sent Slim on another run for more crack. I accepted and I left with him. We smoked up all the money he had plus all the money he had given me and then all the money from his account through the ATM. Now we were busted and we were getting low on gas for his car. We were sitting under a tree one day just thinking about our next move. He looked at me just as serious as ever and said , "I think I love you." He said, " you're beautiful." He knew I needed clothes so he said, " you know what ? I'm going to go to my ex-wife's house and steal all of her clothes and give them all to you." I said, "hell no! I don't want her clothes are you stupid?" He probably thought that was a sweet thing to say or do but I did not.

Chapter 19 (Running From the Police)

His next thought was to go break into some houses. He said he was going to do all the work and that all I had to do was keep an eye out. I was supposed to make a loud noise if someone came home, so that he would hear it and know to get out or hide. So I agreed and we jumped in the car and took off. He said he knew a neighborhood where the people had money. He drove to a nice looking neighborhood. It was some where in Port Orange. We just casually road through the neighborhood until he saw a house that looked suitable for him. He parked the car and told me that if someone came home to start up a conversation with them and talk loud enough for him to hear. I agreed and he went up to the house. I guess he made a small knock on the door to be sure that no one was home. I couldn't see him but I know he entered the home and shortly afterwards he came out with a lot of jewelry, some electronics and some money. Of course you know we smoked a lot that night. We later sold the jewelry and continued to smoke. After everything was gone we simply went and did another one. But on the third attempt, we pulled up and parked in the driveway but the driveway wasn't close to the house. Maybe this was a town house or something but the driveway was a lot farther back from the house. Mark gets out and goes up to the house. Just from the way the house sits with a whole lot of bushes around it, I couldn't see Mark at all. I was sitting in the car keeping watch as usual. I could hear Mark making loud noises. I guess he was having trouble getting in so he was banging on something. Then this big red pick-up truck pulled up beside our car and parked. I got very nervous so I started talking to her. I'm talking in a loud voice hoping that Mark will hear me and get out. "Hi, how are you?" I said . "It's a pretty nice day out today ha?" She said "oh yes it is, I'm enjoying it so much I'm about to go to the beach." Then she must have seen Mark cause she yelled, "some body's breaking in my house!" Then she looked at me and said "and you're with him that's why you're talking to me!" At that time her daughter must have come out cause then she said "call the police Sheryl, they're breaking into our home!" Then Mark tried to run past the woman across the lawn but she was a very big and tall woman and she just stuck her arm out as he tried to run past her and instantly he was knocked backwards and then they just started fighting in the front yard. The whole while I was trying to drive off but the car was a stick shift and I did not know how to drive a stick shift yet so the car just kept jerking and shutting off. I had jumped from the passenger seat to the driver seat so fast that I left my shoes that I had taken off earlier on the passenger side of the car and when I realized that I was not going to be able to drive that car away from there, I just jumped out of the car and took off running barefoot. By the time I got to the entrance were I could see down the other street I saw a long line of police cars speeding towards me. I was so scared that I just ran straight across the street and into the woods.

I was barefoot but I didn't care. I just wanted to get away. So I was running through a very thick wooded area. It was so thick that it provided a good cover for me. I ran and ran and I could hear the sirens the whole time. It seemed like the whole Port Orange police department was after me. I was so scared but I was not going to give up. I ran until I came upon a house deep in the woods and the people were coming out of the house. I could hear their dogs barking and I asked them if I could use their phone, but they looked at me, then looked at each other, then back to me and shook their heads no at the same time. So I ran on further into the woods. I kept running and running. I don't know if I was stepping on splendors or glass or anything that could harm my feet, I just kept running no matter what. Then after what seemed like an eternity, I came upon the back of another house. I could still hear the sirens and the dogs so I run to a bush on the side of the house and stopped to listen. I heard the sound of a car engine racing my way. Something told me to stay behind this bush to see if the car coming was a police car. Sure enough it was. After it passed, the quietness assured me that nothing else was coming. I peeped out to see if there was anyone who could possibly help me. I saw a woman taking her garbage out so I ran over to her and asked her if she would let me use her phone to call me a ride because (immediately I made up a lie),I said, " a man saw me walking and offered me a ride but when I got in the car he tried to rape me so I jumped out and ran, so that is why I don't have on any shoe's." She believed me and felt sorry for me and even though she couldn't give me a ride she did let me use her phone. We went inside and I called my aunt Eva Lee's house cause I knew Rachel, my cousin's girlfriend, would be there. She was there but did not have her car and couldn't come get me. The woman felt so bad for me that she told me her next door neighbor was about to leave for work and she would ask her to give me a ride. So she did and the neighbor said sure. She felt sorry for me too after she heard the story. She gave me a ride from Port Orange to the corner of Mason ave. and Clyde Morris. I was so happy I said , "Thank you God!" At that time the area on the other side of Mason Ave. was all woods. So I ran across the street, into the woods and came in through the back of the creek. It was home sweet home and I was so happy.

Chapter 20 (Making a Change for the Better)

I think that incident scared me so bad that I asked God to please help me to get off of crack. I called Bernard and told him to bring my baby back to me at my Aunt Eva Lee's house and that's where I stayed. I went over to talk to my friend Michelle to let her know what I had just went through and that I was tired of living that way. I told her that I wanted to get away. We both agreed that if we could go far away from here that we could get off crack. So the next day in the scorching hot sun we walked from the creek to the unemployment office. It was located on Seagrave, the same street my mom lived at with the rats in the house. That's a distance of about five miles. We were desperate and parched when we got there. We wanted to go to the Job Corp. I asked that woman to send me as far away from Daytona as she could and she said, " the farthest I can send you is Morganfield, Ky. I said, "sign me up," and Michelle did too. We were ready to go and willing to not smoke any more crack. I promised God that if he sent me away that I would not smoke crack any more. Michelle went to the Job Corp.

before me because I had to get my baby situated first. Then I left after her but we both went to the same place . It was nice. It was a good change in my life. When I got on that Grey Hound Bus, it was such an exhilarating feeling that I never thought about crack ever again. I actually felt like I was some body. I believe from me asking God to help me to get off of crack, that he answered my prayers by taking the urge completely away from me. When you sincerely, from the bottom of your heart, pray and ask God for something that he knows that we truly want to depend on him and trust in him because we recognize his mighty powers and his unchanging love for us. That's when God does great works in our lives. When I got to the Earl C. Clements Job Corp. Center I devoted myself to my studies and made a complete turn around in my life. It was winter time and extremely cold when I got there. I was not prepared for this kind of winter, and there was a snow blizzard on the way. I barely had enough clothes to get me through one week and none of it was snow blizzard material. I caught the flu immediately. I had to go to the medic ward called sick hall. When they took my weight, I only weighed ninety nine pounds. My chest and butt was completely flat from smoking crack so long. I stayed in the medic ward for almost a week before I got well enough to come back to the dorm. It took them about three days to get my temperature down. I had the shakes, my whole body was hurting and aching and I had no appetite and no strength. It was bad, I kept harking up this thick, brown and black looking stuff. I don't know if it was from the flu or withdrawals from all that crack I had smoked before I got there. I'm unsure but they worked on me until I was all better. The dorms had four wings and every wing had at least four to eight rooms with at least six girls to every room. There were boy dorms too but they were quite a distance away from the girls dorms. Every room was assigned a dorm duty and every person had to keep their own quarters clean. One room may have the shower room to keep clean. Every one on each wing shared one shower room that had about six shower heads in an open shower area. One room may be responsible for the T.V. room where one whole wing shared one television. Another room would have to buff and dust mop the hallway and the other room would have the utility room and lobby area of that wing. All these duties had to be performed daily and they were done before breakfast. Breakfast was served at six A.M., and we had to stand in long lines outside the cafeteria, either in the freezing cold or in the scorching sun. There were a lot of kids there and the center was huge. After breakfast was over everyone went to class. In class we focused on our G.E.D. or a skill of our own choice. There were a lot of skills to choose from. At first I chose welding but that was a mistake cause there are little fire sparks during welding jobs and I was afraid of that. I got out of that and entered business clerical. I got my G.E.D. within the first two months of being there. Then I began working on my skill. Learning to type was interesting and I really enjoyed it, therefore I worked very hard everyday. Once I learned the keyboard I built up my speed and before I knew it I was typing up to forty words per minute. I was really starting to feel important. I was really feeling like I can do anything. I knew it was God but from that moment and even now I know through Christ I was able to do anything I wanted to do and anything I tried to do after that God has made all possible. Life was wonderful, and the center had everything we could possibly need. I never had to leave that center for anything. They had a Chapel, a hospital, a campus jail, a campus store, a snack bar, a recreation hall, classes and a library and post office. Some things were in long distances but everything you needed was there on the center grounds. At first one of my roommates didn't like me for some reason. Her name was Melissa. I didn't have any more than she did except the fact that she was there longer than I was, and she always used that against me. She would say "look at you, you ain't got no days, you're a new jack." Because she knew I didn't have many clothes so she would come to my closet, open both doors wide and say "hello…..hello…..hello…"as if to cause an echo, suggesting I had no clothes in my closet just to humiliate me in front of the rest of our roommates. Then she would just laugh her big head off. Yes it was very embarrassing but I was thankful for what I had. My cousin Daphne had given me the little clothes that I had from her aunt Rita who was going to throw the clothes in the garbage. Daphne, knowing I had nothing and was about to go to the Job Corp. where it was very cold, out of the sympathy of her sweet heart, asked if she could give them to me and I was very thankful for both the clothes and my cousins love. Daphne was also the only person to right me from home except my little sister Tammie wanting to know if she was supposed to let boys touch her breasts. I was gone a whole year and Daphne stayed in touch with me the whole time. A short time after I got there my clothing allotment came through and I was able to go buy clothes from the campus store. Everyone was entitled to an allotment when you first got to job corp. I desperately needed mine and I used it immediately. My friend Michelle went with me to the store to show me how everything was set up and I bought every thing I needed. The campus store had everything from clothes and boots and coats to school supplies. After my shopping spree I was ready for the winter. I had to get prepared because we had to walk to all our classes in the snow blizzard. I had boots, long johns, coats, hats, gloves, earmuffs and scarfs cause when the snow lands on you it melts and leaves you wet. I did not want to be sick again so I bundled up for the winter. When I came back to my dorm to put my things away it was almost dark so Michelle just went to her dorm. Melissa had already saw Micelle leave after helping me to the dorm with my things cause she was standing outside the dorm with her boyfriend when we walked up. I guess Melissa got jealous or something cause when her boyfriend left, she came inside with an attitude. She said something smart to me and I said something back cause I was tired of her shit, and I was ready for whatever. I had just earlier that week saw a girl hit another girl in the head with an iron, so I already knew not to fight fair. When the other roommates saw that I wasn't backing down from her they grabbed her and tried to pull her out of the room but she grabbed a ceramic bog from the desk and threw it at me. I tried to bend down but it hit me any way, right on the left side of my chin. When It hit me it damaged my tooth somehow and still to this day that tooth bothers me sometimes. They hauled us both off to time out, the center's jail where we spent one night and was released. After a few months had went by I had completed the world of work program and had become a teachers aide. I had to help the teacher grade papers and then help any students that didn't understand. Melissa was in that class. She had been at the center for at least a year and had not even acquired her G.E.D. She had not completed a skill yet and she had not even completed the world of work program either. Now she wanted to be my friend after I had to help her to understand her work but she never did complete her skill and nothing else and she was later terminated. During my stay at the Job Corp., I met a guy named Johnny whom I thought I was going to marry. He was a nice looking young man. He had a nice build and he was an average size man. He had long braids that were past his shoulders. I was crazy about him as soon as I saw him. I think he was a teacher's aid too and that's how I met him. We started talking and we realized we both liked each other and we started dating. He used to come to my dorm after school and we would go spend the rest of every evening together We would always make it in just before curfew. Sometimes we'd go to the little movie room and we would watch a couple of movies while he tried to get his hands in my pants. We mostly just cuddle and kiss through the whole movie time or some times he would get his hand in my pants and finger me and play in my wet vagina under the cover of his coat. We would always sit all the way in the back of the room and nobody ever knew. When things got too hot and steamy, we would go to the green grass motel. That's what everyone on campus called it when couples would get a blanket and go out to the middle of a certain field of grass, spread their blankets and have sex. We weren't allowed to do this but that's what couples did in order to be together. I would see him from a distance after he had walked me back to my dorm and was then walking back to his dorm I'd see him smelling his fingers and I would yell to him "I see you Johnny" and he would just laugh and throw his arm up in the air as to say "go on inside." Then when I see him the next day he would mock what I said. In a little girlie voice he would say "I see you Johnny." and we'd just laugh and laugh together. He said he loved my smell. Sometimes we would just sit down under a tree and talk about our lives or just about ourselves in general. Or sometimes we would go to the recreation hall called 1501. That was the number of the building so therefore it was the name of the building. There you could play pool, play cards such as spades, table games like ping pong and air hockey. The card tables were lined up alongside the walls on each side of the building. People were always waiting in line to get the next down to play spades. Whoever had themselves a partner could play. It was a lot of fun cause it was always so many people there after class was out everyday. There was snack bar too. That was were you had to go to get all your snacks. All kinds of snack cakes and candy and packages of Ramen noodles etc… Once dinner was over at about six P.M., there was nothing else to eat until five thirty the next morning, unless you had yourself some snacks from the snack bar to sneak and eat late at night. Sometimes you may not have enough snacks to last you and so you just had to stay hungry all night. Some of the girls were doing strange things for snacks and they were later called snack cake whores behind their backs. The boys who knew what the girls had done would ridicule them out loud the next day. It was crazy. There was always a crowd at the snack bar just like at 1501. Everybody knew to be in the dorms by curfew. Everybody except Michelle and some guys she had ran the trail with. Running the trail was sneaking off campus through some wooded area to get to the city. They would run to get liquor. They called the liquor "oil." When they weren't in their dorms at roll call and then later caught coming back onto the center they were terminated. Sent home immediately. I never tried to run the trail because I knew it was wrong and that just wasn't what I went there for. Plus one night while me and Johnny were at the green grass motel, we saw a row of white things from a distance in the dark. We did not know what It was at first but when they got closer we could clearly see that it was the Ku Klutz Klan. They were coming into the field where we were laying so we jumped up and ran as fast as we could back to our dorms. I don't think they did anything that night but we had already been warned upon arrival at the center to stay on campus cause the KKK does roam around in the woods of Kentucky. That was our last time at the green grass motel. I was so scared. Then when Michelle left I was so sad but I knew I had to get what I came for before I left so I studied even harder.

Chapter 21 (Going to New Jersey)

After dating for a while Johnny asked me to transfer my paperwork from Daytona to New Jersey cause he wanted me to come home with him. Even though I knew my responsibility to my daughter was first. Instead I went to New Jersey. Johnny and I had made plans to go get Quala after we both found jobs. Nothing went as planned. Although I did found a job, Johnny got arrested selling cocaine and he had to spend a few nights in the pen. I was very scared and lonely even though his sister was always in the other room. She hardly ever came out of that room so the whole time he was in jail I was alone. They lived in a big two story house. Only Johnny and his sister lived there until I came. Their father always paid the rent but he lived somewhere else. I never had the pleasure of meeting him. At first Johnny was very loving and affectionate. He used to take me on long walks to see the city. We bought his and hers sweaters that were made out of wool and suede. They looked like tiger fur on them. They were different but they were pretty. I saw a lot of homeless people while walking through Newark, New Jersey and nobody seemed to care. We walked by a man laying on a concrete bench in the middle of winter with his pants pulled down to his ankles with a pile of shit behind him and he was fast asleep. It was so cold that it felt like my skin was burning and the man had his backside exposed. I was appalled at the fact that people were just casually walking by as if he wasn't even there. People were lined up in the subways laying on cardboard boxes trying to stay out of the cold. It had to be at least ten degrees out side, maybe lower. I hadn't seen these king of things in Florida, so I felt sorry for the people and I wanted to give them money but Johnny told me no cause they would follow me around if I gave them anything. Another day he took me to Manhattan, New York to see Madison Square Gardens. We walked up and down forty second street and Broadway. While we were walking down forty second street I saw two men tongue kissing each other as if they were man and woman. That was shocking to me. A little further down the road, I saw a man running for his life. There was another man chasing him with a straight blade or razor or something. The man was so tired but the other man was gaining on him so he ran up to a police car that was waiting at the red light and said "help me he's trying to kill me!" The police had his window down about a quarter of the way and he simply let his window up and drove off leaving the man running for his life. The officer did not help at all and that to me was too much. I knew right then that if the police were afraid then there is no where to turn and I decided right then that I would not be raising a family there. It was too fast for me. Soon after that, for some reason Johnny just changed. He got really, really mad at me one day when the grease from the straightening comb melted and ran down to his scalp and burned him. I didn't even want to straighten his hair but he insisted. Therefore he thought I burned him on purpose because I didn't want to do it in the first place., but I didn't. He got so mad at me, that he started yelling and looking crazy, then he took some plates in his hand and one by one, he threw them so hard against the wall that they shattered into many pieces. I couldn't believe it. This behavior was bizarre and it continued right through the night. It was snowing that night and he was still so angry that he let up the window in the room and took all the covers and turned the heater in the room off. He literally tried to freeze me to death so I just simply got up and put on every piece of clothing I had and slept in the living room on the couch. The next morning I woke up early. Before daylight. It must have been about five thirty a.m. I walked to the corner of the street to use the pay phone. I called my Aunt Eva Lee and told her about what he had done. It just so happened that her son, my cousin, Darryl was there and he was kind enough to buy me a bus ticket to get home. He told me to go to the station at day light and I came home immediately. I thank God for my cousin Darryl, he was there for me at the flash of lighting with no questions asked. I appreciated him. Of course I had to make up a lie to tell Johnny cause he was not going to just let me leave just like that. I told him that my aunt sent me a ticket to come get Quala and go back to New Jersey. I left everything I owned except the clothes on my back just to make him believe that I was coming back. Otherwise he would not have let me go. I was wearing two coats when I left and a lot of under clothes, because of the cold there but I knew I wouldn't need all that stuff in Daytona. By me leaving everything Johnny thought I was coming back. I never wanted to see that fool again after that behavior.

Chapter 22 (Back to Daytona)

When I came home I was so happy to see my baby but something was wrong. When I walked in the door she was sitting in a corner and she had this traumatized look on her face. It was as if it was permanently engraved on her face as if she was petrified. Even though I was anxiously ready to see her and hold her and talk to her, the feeling that came over me was eerily strange. Before I went to the Job Corp. she was vibrant with a happy appearance. She was wearing a little yellow outfit when I walked in, I'll never forget and I said "hey mama's sugar!" and she just sat there like she had no clue that I was talking to her or like she was afraid to move because she was made by force to sit still for hours at a time just like the foster kids there. My aunt became a foster mom after all her own kids were grown and gone and I truly loved my Aunt Eva Lee but sometimes she was abusive to kids. By then Quala was two years old and the look on Quala's face made me think about the time when Quala was about two months old and my aunt was beating one of the adopted kids named Lakeisha with a leather strap, trying to make her say a Christmas speech for an upcoming church play. Lakeisha was about four years old. My aunt kept hitting her for at least thirty minutes before I woke up completely. I thought I was dreaming at first and I kept sleeping. When I realized I was not dreaming, I got up to see what was going on. Quala, was laying on a pallet on the floor in my aunt's room while all of this was going on. I burst into the room to find that she had stripped the child naked, she had her youngest biological child holding the adopted child down while she repeatedly whipped the four year old child with a slim leather strap. The child was screaming to the top of her lungs and my aunt kept saying to her "shut your mouth and say that speech! You better say it and get it right! Say it!" she kept saying. I thought for sure that by now the child's but was probably lacerated. I felt so much sorrow for that little girl cause she was always getting some kind of abuse from my aunt. I quickly picked up my baby and got out of that house. I walked around the corner to my Aunt Lillie Mae's house to tell her about the abuse that I had just witnessed. I also called my grandmother and told her what was going on and she told me that my auntie would never hurt a child. I also remember an earlier occasion when Aunt Eva Lee wet a hand towel and beat one of the white foster kids with it because that way the kids would not bruise. There were other things too but this just showed me what kind of things she would do, which made me know that she had been beating my two year old daughter too. She just wasn't responding to me as she should have like most babies who have not seen their mother in a long time. So I just took her away quietly. I didn't say anything at all about my suspicions. We went to stay with my cousin Daphne because she offered to let us stay until I got my own place. That was another blessing from God.

Chapter 23 (A Thief in the Night)

During my stay with Daphne is when my cousin Red, started breaking into all the apartments around the complex. It was a small apartment complex with about 30 to 40 apartments, all connected together in the shape of a square with a pool in the center. It was a nice place to live but all the apartments had sliding glass doors and balconies on some of them which made it easier to break in upstairs or downstairs. Red broke into almost all of the apartments and took whatever he could find. He even broke into Daphne's place, his own sister, whenever he wanted to feed his crack habit, which was constantly except while he was smoking. One night very late, while we were sleeping, something just woke me up out of a deep sleep which is unusual because I sleep very hard. It must have been the Lord again but I woke up to pitch black darkness and I heard movement so I knew someone was there. I focused really hard until my eyes adjusted enough to see his eyes and his body shape. When he would brake in, he would crawl around on his hands and knees to move around your whole house and take whatever he could. He would knock lightly on your door so that if you were awake you would hear him and answer but if you were asleep you would not hear it. If no one answered he knew you were asleep then he quietly breaks in whether you're home or not. So when I focused and saw that it was someone, of course I was scared because he was lying there looking at me, and I'm looking at him on the floor and all I could see was the white of his eyes. So I yelled "Who is that?!" Then he said "It's me Trece Ann, Red." Then I realized what was going on because he was almost to my purse. He was crawling around on his belly like a snake, stealing people's money and anything of value to sell for crack. I said "Get the fuck out of here Red. Stealing from your own family." I can't remember if I woke Daphne up right then or if I told her the next morning but when I told her she went to check her purse. Only to find that he had stolen all of her food stamps leaving her and her kids without food for a month. After a few weeks, the apartment manager knew that Daphne's brother was the person responsible for all these break ins, but it kept happening until they finally just told Daphne to move out.

Chapter 24 (Another Psycho)

By then I had received my check from the Job Corp. and was able to get my own place out there. I was so happy to have my very own place for the first time in my life. My baby and I had a place to call "home". As soon as I got the place, my friend Eric, whom I met through my friend Michelle, bought me a microwave. It was the only thing I had in my apartment and as soon as I left to go get more things someone came inside my apartment and stole the microwave. When we put the microwave in the apartment there were some people upstairs who saw us take it inside and then they also saw us leave afterwards, so I don't know if they stole it or if my cousin Red stole it. Eric was Michelle's nephew. She said I should get with him because he had money and I could get it if I was his girlfriend. Even though I did not like him and was not attracted to him, I felt the need to get with him to get my apartment furnished and he did furnish it. He bought me a king size waterbed that stood about four feet off the ground with dresser drawers built around the sides of it and a mirror and lights in the headboard. He bought me a chest drawer dresser with two large doors that opened outward on the top and had three large drawers on the bottom and it matched the waterbed., so it was a set. He brought me a living room set and a twin bed set for my daughter's room. He was very nice at first. Then one day he just didn't come to my house. Then the next day he didn't come again, so I didn't know what was going on but I was glad. I was glad that he wasn't trying to come around me because I really didn't like him and did not want him to touch me either, but to get what you want you have to give up a little something and I hated every minute of being with him. A few days passed and then he came back with hickies all over his neck, and he told me that he had been with this girl named Monique who works at the Texaco Gas Station . So now this news makes me happy and I told him congratulations . I was actually happy, so then I ask him "Why are you here?" He said he just wanted to tell me. So I said "OK go have fun", and he left. But he came back the next day, and I guess he was mad because I didn't get mad about him being with Monique. He had someone in the car with him and he asked me to ride with him to drop this guy off. I said "O.K." and when the guy got out of the car, Eric makes up some bogus story about me and another guy and all of a sudden he punched me really hard in my face. It was a very painful blow. It felt like he had pushed my nose into my head. My eyes watered up and I couldn't talk, breath or see. I'll never forget that blow. After a few weeks Bernard come to see Quala. One thing led to another and he said he wanted to stay the night and take care of us. So I thought it was the right thing to do, since he was Quala's father, so I let him stay. After Quala was asleep, we went into my room and began doing what grownups do. Then there was a knock at the window. At first I thought it was my cousin Karen, or my friend Michelle, but something told me not to say anything, and I told Bernard not to say anything. So the knocks continued and then finally in a low voice some one said "Trece!" which let me know it was Eric. I knew his voice, but why would he come here when we agreed he could stay with Monique. I'm unsure of why he came but he did and I wouldn't answer the door so he left. But only to go to the Bottom and get Michelle and he punched her in her face and made her come back with him to see if I would open the door for her. We didn't know that he was with her, we thought it was Michelle who needed me to open the door for her because at that time, she was living with me. So when Michelle called my name Bernard said "Yeah?" and Eric heard him. All before, Eric didn't know I was in there until Bernard said something. When Eric knew we were inside, he ran around to the kitchen door, which had a window in the center of it and he punched through the window and stuck his hand inside and unlocked the door and came into my apartment. Since we thought he was gone the first time we continued having sex. This caused me to still be undressed when Eric walked in. Bernard had a gun in his hand but he was afraid to use it, even to just hit Eric with it. Eric walked right up to Bernard and took his gun from him. That's when I took off running. I had a towel around me when I ran out the door and down the street. Eric started running behind me. When I looked back and saw him chasing me, I dropped the towel and picked up speed. I ran down to Daphne's house because she wasn't completely moved out yet because they gave her thirty days to be gone. Bernard ran to his sister's house who lived in the same complex but around on the other side. He came back with his sister like a scared child who runs to get his bigger brother instead of fighting his own battles. That was a very embarrassing scene of me running naked down the street while a man chases me wanting to hurt me, but that's exactly how it happened. It was so much commotion that it woke up some neighbors and they were standing outside watching and someone called the police. But Eric left before they got there. This whole thing was just senseless jealousy on Eric's behalf and after seeing Bernard's weakness I never ever messed with him anymore. I had learned a valuable lesson that night, which is if a man can't protect you, you don't need to be with him. After that, I prayed that God would send me a man-just for me. A man who would love me for me and who would treat me the way a woman should be treated.

Chapter 25 (Meeting My Husband)

Michelle and Karen moved in with me just in case Eric came back cause I was to scared.

As time went on they began disrespecting my apartment by inviting their boyfriends over, letting them spend the night and Karen took showers with her man, with no regards for my child or how she was perceiving all of this. My apartment was only a two bedroom, one bathroom apartment and they wouldn't even help me keep it clean. Then they just stopped helping pay the rent. I decided we should all go look for a job together before the rent was due for the next month. All of us were unemployed but I had money left over from my Job Corp. check but I knew it would not be enough to pay the rent by myself as I had been doing. The next morning Michelle and I set out to find a job. I wanted to get a job within walking distance of my place because neither one of us had a car. We went to the linen service first because it was the closet. We went in and filled out the application and the man told us we were hired; just like that he told us to report for work at 7:00 pm that night. We were assigned to the soil room which is where all the soiled linen comes in and our job was to count each piece and separate them. It was things like sheets from hospitals and napkins and bar towels from restaurants. Sometimes the sheets from the hospitals would be blood stained and full of afterbirth or the restaurant linen may have old rotten food such as breadstick. That stuff smelled so bad that it used to make me gag every night when I walked in to work. The reason I was gagging was because I was pregnant. I didn't find this out until just before I started working there. As soon as I found out I knew I was not going to keep it. One night at work one of the guys from the soil room, who worked right behind me on the belt line, walked pass me and said something but I didn't hear him. I asked him what did he say but he just kept walking. He was a handsome man. Even though he was a big man, he was very attractive. He had the most beautiful skin and complexion that I had ever seen on a black man. He looked really clean too, like he took really good care of his skin. I notice these things on a man because my skin is not so great. He was wearing a red shirt, a pair of red shorts, and some red converses, Chuck Taylor's, everyone was wearing them back then. I decided I wanted him. He must have wanted me too because he asked his friend, who worked right beside him on the belt, about me and he took one look at me and told him "She's pregnant." His friend, named Reggie, already knew me from growing up in the creek with me, so I guess my face looked fat to him or something but he was right. I went ahead and admitted it when he asked me but I told him that I wasn't planning on keeping the baby. His name was Terrence Bell but everyone called him T.Bell, for short. He said he still liked me even though I was pregnant. He asked me to go home with him after work the next morning. I said yes. When we got off, he was gone. I felt strange but I thought maybe he was just playing when he asked me to come home with him. So the next night at work, he asked me to go home with him again, and again, when we got off, he was gone. So the next night at work, I asked him "What's wrong with you, and why do you ask me to go if you know you're just going to leave without me?" He said he was scared and he thought I was going to try to take over his house. He had just moved into his place too but it was a house, not an apartment. When he told me why he was scared, I just laughed and laughed. I said "Boy, I don't want to take over your place. I have my own place." So after work he was there and he took me back to my place to get some clothes and I went with him to his house. He had his own car, his own place, and a job. I felt like maybe he was the one for me. His house was very clean inside and it had a lovely smell to it. He enjoyed burning incents. Even though they gave off a lovely smell I was allergic to them. After being closed in to long with them my eyes would start burning. His house was so clean that I thought his mother lived there with him. So I did a complete search of the house and to my surprise there were no signs of a woman at all. I felt more comfortable knowing he lived alone. In his bedroom, he alternated between a blue light or a red light but both were sexy and exotic. He had a round table in his room that had all his hats on it. He loves wearing hats. With each hat there was an outfit and a pair of shoes to match. He had the most expensive colognes that I had ever smelled on a man. He had a stereo in his house but no television. He had a tray full of marijuana but no food. I indulged with the weed and when we were hungry we went to Gooding's grocery store and bought us some food and cooked us some breakfast. He said he hadn't had one of those in a while. After my shower I slipped into one of his T-shirts and no panties. He had the blue light on that night and we were both ready for each other. He had some slow music playing and we just fell in love with each other. His body and his skin felt so smooth against mine. We caressed and kissed each other ever so slowly and sincerely. He was touching and rubbing me in all the right places. The music was truly love making music and everything was so good and beautiful. Even though he was a little premature, I knew we would stay together. We just had to get used to each other and learn each other's bodies. He said he hadn't been with a woman in over a year, so I knew it would get better and it did. The next time was better and the next time even better than that time. We were in love. T.Bell offered to help me pay for an abortion. He took me to the place and gave me the money and waited for me, then drove me home. He was there for me every step of the way and I appreciated him for that. He went out of town one time and came back with all these gifts for me. It made me feel so special because no one had ever bought me a gift before. He bought me a necklace, two bracelets, some earrings and three outfits. Back then he was trafficking cocaine back and forth to Miami to Daytona and getting paid for it, but I did not know at that time what he was doing. We dated about a year after that when I got pregnant from T.Bell. This news was great because he was told by doctors that he would never be able to have a child because his sperm count was to low from a previous hernia in his testes. He had the hernia removed but they said chances were still low. This all happened before he met me so I believed he couldn't have kids so we had unprotected sex all the time, because he wanted a child real bad. When the good Lord above was ready, he blessed us with a fetus in the womb. T.Bell was so happy. His family was happy too. Quala was happy to know she was going to have a sister or brother. She was almost four, with no playmate. At that time I was working across the river as a maid, and T.Bell had stopped working at the linen service and was slanging and taking trips. Things were kinda hard but God always made a way. They had just come out with a new bath soap on the market and they were giving everyone free samples through the mail. Sense there was an empty house two doors down from us T.Bell decided he wanted me to go down to the empty house and get the bar of soap from the mailbox. When I refused he got mad. I don't know why wouldn't he go down himself and get the bar of soap. He asked me again to go get it and when I said no again he grabbed me around the neck and started choking me. Of course I was trying to get away from him but he was too strong. I thought he was going to choke the life right out of me, but the white man who lived next door saw what was going on and ran out there to stop him. We were in the front yard so that's how the man saw us but T.Bell's best friend named Paul was sitting there in the living room and did not say a word or lift a finger to help me. He didn't like me from the beginning and he probably thought that I was pregnant from someone other than T.Bell. When we first got together I heard Paul say, with my own ears to T.Bell that I'm just a whore and he shouldn't be with me. So I guess that's why he didn't try to get T.Bell off me when he was choking me he just sat there like nothing was going on. I thank God for that white man.

Chapter 26 (God Sent me a Son)

Everything was well and fine, I gave birth to a healthy baby boy on February 4, 1991. This was my second child born on the fourth day of the month. Quala was born October 4, 1986. When I went into labor T.Bell was so nervous. He drove me to the hospital so fast, that I thought surely we were going to get pulled over by the police but we didn't. Unlike Bernard, T.Bell was there through the entire pregnancy. His mom and dad were also there. The labor was hard and long and I could see the sorrow and concern on T.Bell's face. He was scared to. After all those hours of watching the monitor that was attached to my stomach and letting me know each time a contraction was coming, it was almost time for the actual birth. I had dilated all ten centimeters and the doctor told me to push. I took in a deep breath and pushed with all my might and my son's head popped out. T.Bell saw that and he took off running. They had to go and get him. He had ran all the way to the elevators. I knew this was going to be scary for him because he had never seen child birth before. He said all the blood made him sick. We had a healthy baby boy and we named him Terrence Demetrius Bell Jr., after his father. We call him Terry for short. Some time during the pregnancy I had been given a voucher from Section 8, which is a housing agency and I got my own apartment in Hillcrest. T.Bell and I were together but he had his own place and I had my own place. We would just spend the night back and forth at each other's house but we never slept apart. Then when my son was close to a year old T.Bell got busted on a road trip down in Fort Lauderdale and it was the Feds. not local enforcement. I knew something was wrong when it got really late and he was not home yet. He never used to stay gone this long. Then morning came and he had not come home yet. I remember a very lonely and sad feeling come over me and the only person there with me was my son. Quala was over to her grandmother's house. Bernard's mother. At about 7am there was a knock on the door. I already knew something was wrong but I didn't know what. I had thoughts of him having an accident and no one knowing about it or where he was. It was Sharon, Paul's wife. She came to tell me that T.Bell had been arrested in Ft. Lauderdale and that we had to wait for him to call so we would know what was going on. It was awful, I felt like my whole world was shattered. I just held Terry real tight and cried. I was devastated. After I pulled myself together I went to Paul's house to wait for T.Bell to call because he didn't have a phone at his house. He finally called and told us what his bond was and what his charges were. They did not get any drugs off him because he had already given the guy the money but the guy had not come back yet with the drugs but they new somehow he was involved because he had just gotten out of the truck with the man who had the money at the time of the bust. They held T.Bell down there in jail for three weeks before they were forced to drop the charges due to lack of evidence and let him go. We all were so happy. I was so scared because they were talking about giving him ten years at first. So he was given a second chance at life. When he was in jail he had told me about some ring he had for me and he was planning on asking me to marry him. I felt like it was just jail house talk because I had never seen the ring. He just told me that if he got out of that place that he was going to propose to me, but I was not ready for marriage so we just stayed together as boyfriend and girlfriend. Most of the time it was sweet until times when T.Bell would do something involving Quala that would either make me sad or mad. Like sometimes he would fix her a bowl of cereal that he knew she wouldn't like and make her sit there for hours trying to force her to over eat when he knew she would only eat very small portions. She had to sit there and keep her head forward, he did not allow her to turn her head either way while she was eating. This is how she had to sit on the couch too while watching T.V. He had her scared to turn her head even when someone came into the house. She had to sit there for hours or he would let her go play with her toys in the closet. It was a walk in closet and that's where she had to play at. Some of his friends would call Quala "closet child" in a joking way, but it always made me feel bad as a mother. He never did hit her or anything it was mostly just mental abuse. Sometimes he was nice to her. He brought her a bicycle and gave her the first birthday party she had ever had. It was when she turned three years old. When Terry was born T.Bell didn't want her close to the baby. He said he didn't want her to breath on him because he was a newborn. Then, whenever Quala would get close to the rails of his crib T.Bell would say back-up. So I used to let Quala spend a lot of time at her grandmother's house with her daddy and his people, because I knew that over there she could relax and just be a kid. Even though every time she came home I would have to take her straight to the bath tub. She was always very dirty by the time she came home but she loved to go over there. When she came home

I could always see the expression change in Quala and in T.Bell when she walked through the door. She came home with a little play make-up set that had some bracelets with it, and as soon as she came in the house he took it away from her and we never saw it again. Her Uncle Willie had bought it for her and as soon as they left T.Bell took it from her and said, "she don't need to have all that grown and fast shit. She is to bad already." He used to tell me all the time that she was going to grow up to be this terrible person who was definitely going to embarrass and disrespect me one day. Those things he said hurt me and I would cry at night and then he would get in bed wanting to have sex with me. The hardest thing to do is to have sex with the person that's hurting your child's feelings and most of the time I would not do it. Not all things were bad, he did some things to make me happy, like when he threw me a surprise birthday party. He invited all my cousins and all of our friends and it was great. It was such a surprise, I didn't even realize it was my party. He had told me that he was going to take me out to dinner and to the movies and that we were going to the movies first. The name of the movie we were going to see was called "The Texas Chainsaw Massacre," it was one of my favorites. I love scary movies and T.Bell knew that. I was so excited that I walked right past the people that were coming into our house for the party. When I saw the cake then I realized it was my party. I was ecstatic and embarrassed, but overall It was great. We've taken family trips before with our kids and our friends Paul and Sharon or Reggie and Denise. Two of T. Bell's good friends and their wives. We took our kids to Busch Gardens about three times, Sea world once, Six Flags and White Water Rapids. We used to have lots of fun most of the time.

Chapter 27 (Becoming a Certified Nurses Assistant)

When Terry was about a year old, I began working as a Certified Nurse's Assistant in a local nursing home. My cousins, Michelle and Daphne, told me about this kind of work and they told me to come fill out an application and I could get a job. I went and put in a application and they hired me. I lied and said that I was registered to take the C.N.A. class and the Director of Nurses named Ann Marie hire me. With no training at all, I was working as a C.N.A. Daphne showed me what to do and I learned it very well. I worked there for almost two years before State Board came in and said that everyone must be State Board Certified to work there. So I went and challenged the test at Daytona State College and passed it and I received my license. There were a few people working there that I already knew but then I met a lot of people that I had never seen before. My duties consisted of caring for the elderly. We were responsible for feeding them, bathing them, making their beds, taking their vital signs, documenting their food & liquid intake and output. Me and Daphne worked together as a team in our group. It was easier working together then alone because you never had to go look for help. The nurses made our assignment sheets out and sometimes each C.N.A. could have anywhere from fifteen to twenty two patients on the three to eleven shift and any where from ten to fifteen patients on the seven to three shift. This is due to being understaffed. The facility was always understaffed which in turn leaves the residents of the facility with inadequate care. Residents are supposed to be repositioned every two hours and changed if they are incontinent or do not have a cathedar and foley bag. They have to be fed twice on day shift and once on evening shift. If we did not have enough C.N.A.'s then we just worked with what we had and did the best that we could do. If there were only three aids to a wing then none of the residents could get proper care. They were lucky to just got fed and put to bed with a bed bath. No showers are possible if each C.N.A. had a whole hall of people to take care of. The amount of work was to great for one person to take care a whole hall. A whole hall consist of about twenty-two people. Each one wanting to go to bed right after dinner. Eventually the lack of staffing pushed me away from that job but we made the best of it and laughed when we could. Some of the patients were very funny. I grew to love them. I learned a lot from the elderly too. We treated each person as if they were either our grandmother or grandfather and they learned to love us too. Most people think that nurses or doctors are the ones the patients enjoy but most of the time it's the C.N.A. because that's the on that bonds with them. That's the one that learns how they like their coffee or tea and fixes it and brings it to them every day. The person that's always there to help clean them up if they have an accident and make their bed to make the room look cheery and sometime to put butter and jelly on their toast or even feed them if they can't hold the spoon or fork steady enough to feed themselves. Just listening to them as they tell us how things were in their days when they were young. These were some interesting stories to me and I enjoyed learning from them. I treated all the residents with kindness and respect even when they were not my assigned residents. If they needed something I would get it no matter what or if it was something their aid needed to know I would get their aid for them. Daphne had a very unique sense of humor about herself and everyone loved to be around her. We joked and laughed with the residents who were able to joke and laugh just to pass the day. It used to be so much fun. One day Daphne and I were working together and a man was sitting there who needed to be pulled up in his wheelchair cause he slumped down so far that he was about to slide out onto the floor. So when we got ready to pull him up, Daphne was standing in front of him and she was a pretty heavyset woman. The resident was a black man who used to be a principal and he was just one of our favorites. So he lifts his head up and takes a good look at Daphne and says "wooo woooo, good Lord how much do you weigh three hundred!" He said "you look like a big old barrel!" I t was so funny and unexpected that Daphne had to laugh too. I remember another man who we thought was dying and every time his heart stopped and they tried to revive him, he would always come back to life just in time to grab the nurse's breast. We'd all joke and say he wasn't going to die until he got that last shot of ass. He was about one hundred and two years old but he just would not die. When we would come in to work in the morning time to get him up and ready for breakfast, most of the time he'd have his back turned to the door and he would not answer when you called his name. So Daphne said I know what will get him up. She went and stood in his face, called his name and when he opened his eyes, she lifted her shirt and started shaking her breasts in his face and that would get him up at attention every time. He'd sit straight up in bed with his eyes wide open wanting to see some action. Then he would start making these noises of excitement as if he really wanted to touch her breasts so badly but he couldn't. It was so funny we'd just laugh and laugh. It was sad that it was the quickest way to get him up and it never failed. Even when we were short staffed we would just team up and get the job done. All C.N.A.'s weren't as nice as Daphne and myself. Some C.N.A.'s were bad ones. I have seen some of them bringing pure torture to these residents and that's wrong. The residents pay a lot of money to live in these facilities. I have witnessed residents having their nose, nipples or even ears pinched so hard that they stay red for hours and hours. These are people that are in their golden years being tortured by people that are in there thirties and forties. One thing my grandmother taught me is to always no matter what, respect your elders. These devilish C.N.A.'s did not respect their elders at all. In fact I saw an aide over a period of about seven months time repeatedly tell a resident that she and the residents husband were having an affair. The woman was admitted into the facility for mental problems so for her to be told upsetting things such as this all the time, It literally drove her over the edge. It was causing this woman's blood pressure to go up, causing her mental problems to progress and this C.N.A. just fed off of this so much that she would go into detail about what her and the woman's husband was doing just to further insult the lady. She would tell her these things while she was bathing her because they were assigned to each other. Which made it so easy for her to ultimately run this lady crazy. She would whisper in her ear as she bathed her saying things like "you see these towels I'm using on you, these are the same towels that Joe, the woman's husband, and I used after we got finished fucking" The woman would get so annoyed that

112

one time she ran away from her so fast that she hit her arm on the branch of a fake tree and tore a large area of skin backwards on her arm. It was bleeding pretty bad so they had to bandage it up and she was so agitated that they had to give her a shot of adavan to calm her down. That it usually puts them to sleep. I felt bad and I used to tell the aide to stop but she would just continue and I never reported her because she was my ride back and forth to work. This went on unnoticed for a while. It had become her favorite past time at work. It was fun to her and finally the woman had a stroke. She couldn't walk anymore or even get out of bed by herself anymore. She just went down hill and even on her death bed, the C.N.A., would still go whisper those kinds of things in her ear and you could see a physical change in her even though she could not move or talk. She would just violently shake. The nurses never found out what was the reason why she was peaceful when this aide was not there but combative when she was there. There were other residents that where abused by her and by her friend. There were two of them. One man was very hard to shower or to get him ready for bed so when ever he gave them hard time they would pinch his nipples very, very, hard. He'd yell and fight back but it was two of them and he was n a wheelchair. He could not walk. On his shower nights if he didn't cooperate, they would put him in the shower and turn the cold water on him. Even in the winter time they would do this and once it caused him to catch pneumonia. He almost died from those cold showers. I've seen them leave that man in there for over thirty minutes before. He could not talk which made It so much easier for them to do whatever they wanted to him. Another woman was being mentally abused about her son. She was being told that he was a woman cause he had a sex change. That statement alone used to make that lady so mad she used to try to fight any one she got her hands on. It didn't matter if you weren't the one who actually said or did it, she just wanted someone to take revenge out on. The lady only had one son and so she was really attached to him and she did not like anyone making false accusations about her only child. Her son used to come see her at least three times a week and every time he left they started in with the sex change comments until she had to be medicated. They aggravated her so bad one day that she just took off running and when she dashed out into the hallway she ran right into another resident, a woman who was just walking by and they collided so hard that the woman who was just passing by was knocked to the floor and she broke her hip and never walked again. That was horrible. That innocent woman never recovered from that broken hip and she just went down hill until she died. These kind of things go on every day in nursing homes. There are good C.N.A.'s and there are bad ones but the sad thing is that one day we are all going to need some body to come and see about us when we are to old to see about ourselves. It is a blessing from God to even be able to reach those golden years so remember what ever you do to others will one day come back and happed to you so be careful how we treat our elders.

Chapter 28 (My Best Friend Died in Jail)

During my time of working in this facility I got pregnant with my third child, I got married and my best friend died in jail. All my coworkers arranged a baby shower for me. It was a surprise and I was truly amazed and extremely thankful. I had never had a baby shower before and it was nice. I received a lot of gifts which really came in handy. I got almost everything I needed from the baby shower and then our parents said we were not going to keep having children out of wed lock. A lot happened in the same year. One morning after T.Bell had dropped me off at work, he was pulled over and arrested for driving on a suspended drivers license. They took him to jail and would not even allow him to call me and let me know that he could not take the kids to school. My kids were home alone for about five hours before I found out that he never made it back home. That was so nasty of that police officer to not let him even call me so that I could make arrangements for my kids. When they took T.Bell to jail he wasn't even dressed. He was wearing his Pajamas but that did not stop that officer and he didn't give a damn about my kids. After T.Bell got out of jail our parents started planning our wedding. Then I got that dreadful phone call telling me that my best friend Michelle had died in jail. They say that she was pregnant and the baby died inside of her. By the jail not getting her medical attention in time the baby poisoned her system and caused her to hemorrhage to death. It must have been a painful death cause some of her cellmates told us that when she woke up that morning she told them "I'm going to die today yall." They said she was very cold and was having trembles from the fever so they all gave her their blankets but she was still freezing. They said they even tried to call home for her but no one believed that she was sick because Michelle used to tell so many lies that everybody out side the jail thought that she was crying wolf like she had did so many times before. I remember telling Michelle as a child that she should stop lying so much cause one day when you really need some one to believe you they won't, and that's exactly what happened. She got sick and no body believed her and so she died alone with no family or friends. It was a very sad time in my life. She was my dearest and best friend since kindergarten and I still miss her to this day. We went ahead with the wedding and all went well. My dad paid for my dress and our wedding album. T.Bell's mom did all the decorations and she coordinated the whole thing. It was beautiful. The colors where red and white because it was in the month of December. I had eight ladies and he had eight men. The wedding was a big one. The kids were all dressed up. Quala had on her red silk dress and her hair was long with candy curls and Terry had on a three piece suit that we rented and he was running all over the place doing hook slides in the people's suit. That tuxedo was so dirty when we returned it that we had to pay extra. Every one was there except my friend Michelle, my mom and my brothers. A few days before the wedding my brother Bear had just had an accident at the playground that almost put his eye out. His eye was big, black and swollen shut. He could barley see out of it cause it was so swollen. I was deeply sorrowed so I stayed there and laid next to him until he fell asleep. Eventually it healed up completely and he was back to his old self in no time. You can't even tell that anything happened to him at all. By the time I was married on December 17, my grandmother's birthday, in he year 1994. My sister Tammie had three kids and was in her own apartment. She was my Matron of honor and a beautiful one she was. The only thing we did not have was a decent car to ride off into the sunset in. We had a gray Nissan that was so banged up with holes in the floor board and no A.C. that we called "The Grey Goose." We did not want to go on our honeymoon in that so T.Bell's cousin Derrick gave us a ride to the Marriott where we spent our honeymoon. It was so nice. The food was gourmet and we had room service around the clock for at least three or four days. It was beautiful and fit for a King and a Queen but I really could not party because I was pregnant and miserable. We had a lot of gifts and a lot of money from our wedding. My dad kept Quala and Terry for us because T. Bell had did it right. He asked my dad for my hand in marriage just like in the old days and my dad gave him this big speech and then granted his permission and my dad walked me down the isle. My problem was with the reverend. Our wedding pictures tell the story. The reverend did not show up for rehearsal so he did not know our names and we did not even say our vows to one another. I'm unsure if he had ever married any one before cause he just preached a regular sermon. It seemed to me like the Pastor did not know any wedding vows. It was strange and I did not feel like I had just been married. At the reception, one of T.Bell's friends named Joe, simply walked in unannounced and began singing one of Luther Van dross's greatest love songs and it was just as beautiful as if Luther had singed it himself. It was so perfect, that it seemed to fill the room with love. We just looked into each others eyes with so much Love as he sang. He sounded just like Luther and when he was done he had a standing ovation. Everybody was talking about him. They loved him. He simply walked out just as he had walked in. After that we never saw him again.

Chapter 29 (The Death of my Dear Sweet Aunt)

This was a happy time and a sad time. The reason is because my aunt was in the hospital dying from cancer and my cousin Bennie and his girlfriend were about to give birth to their first child and also my cousin pop was in the hospital also from being hit in his head with a metal drawer while serving time in prison for selling drugs. All of this was going on at the same time in the same hospital. It was sad because my aunt, Daphne's mother, was just fine a few months earlier. She went to the doctor one day and he told her that she had cancer and that they had to cut her open to get it out . Shortly after that she died. Pop wasn't able to see his mom because he was in surgery and my aunt wasn't able to see the newborn baby from her youngest son cause she died while they were still in the delivery room which was on the second floor of the same hospital. So it was a very sad time and a happy time but mostly a sad time for all my cousins. We had not expected her to die at such a young age because to us, she was very healthy but that's what happened to her at the age of 46. The same thing also happened to my mom's mother. She was fine and healthy too. My grandmother used to take her morning walk everyday at about six thirty a.m. She did it for years. She lived in the same house for a lot of years and took care of herself. She performed all her household duties herself. For some reason the family decided to move my grandmother from the house she had been living in for about twenty-thirty years, to a house on Verdell Street. She was unable to make the adjustment and like most old people that have been taken from their homes and daily routines, they get sick and die. All those years that she lived on Wallace Street she never even had a cold but as soon as they moved her, we were told that she had cancer. Shortly after that she was dead. The doctors said that she was to old to have surgery. They said that she would not have been able to come out of the anesthesia and that It would have killed her. They also said that if they cut her that the cancer would spread like wild fire. My grandmother was eighty-two years old when she died so I guess that was a good long life. She served the Lord Jesus all her life and I know in my heart that she is present with the Lord and she's extremely happy. That woman taught me a lifetime of morals and values. I thank God for my grandmother putting that first mustard seed of faith in me as a child and it has carried me a long way. She taught me to pray every night before entering bed and pray every morning as soon as your feet touch the floor. Before you do any thing she taught me that you pray first. On the way to her funeral in Dothan, Alabama, it was a beautiful sight because there are a lot of hills in Alabama and our family all followed one another, so it looked like a long line of cars going over hills one by one. For miles all you could see was our family's cars going over hills. My mom was in the back seat hiding behind some hanging clothes, smoking crack off of her crack pipe. I remember being so mad at my mom cause I thought the least she could do was take the day of your mothers funeral off from smoking crack but no it didn't' seem to phase her at all that her mother was dead.

Chapter 30 (Two More Blessings from God)

Shortly after that I gave birth to my third child. I named her Imani Zakiya Bell. We picked her name out of an African Baby Name Book because we thought she was going to be our last child and we wanted her name to have meaning. Her birthday was April 4, 1995. She was the third child to be born on the forth day of the month plus she was born on T.Bell's mother's birthday and me and T.Bell were both born on the 25th day of different months. Imani was so light skinned that I thought something was wrong with her. I did not give natural birth with her because the pain was so great that I asked for an epidural which is why I thought that had something to do with her color. She had just taken after her dad's side of the family and they are very light. Imani was healthy. When I had the epidural it caused T.Bell to faint from the sight of the very needle because it was extremely long. I had never seen a needle that long. The doctors told T.Bell that he must hold me still in a fetal position while the needle went in or I would be paralyzed. I think the responsibility was to great for him cause as soon as he saw the needle entering my back he became weak and he fainted. They used smelly sauce to wake him up again. After that he seemed to be O.K. When we arrived home with her, Quala and Terry were happy to see their new sister. They both just stared at her and then said "why does she look like that!" I said ,"like what?" They said, "why are her eyes so for apart?" I said ,"I don't know" but there's nothing wrong with her that's just how she looks. After about nine months we were pregnant again. We were devastated. Actually we were in shock. I had the doctor to do the pregnancy test again to be sure, and again it said I was pregnant. Times had been rough on us through the previous pregnancy, we didn't think we could afford another child nor could I risk time off work again, because at that time T.Bell was a car detailer. We were having terrible thought s about bringing another baby into our already financially difficult lives. It was so devastating that we considered having an abortion instead of trusting in God. A few days later God blessed T. Bell with a better job working at a printing company. We knew it was an answer from God so we kept our baby. I got a job at a different nursing home facility because that was the best employment opportunities for me due to the excessive overtime. The pay was better and they were well staffed at all times. At that time I was about five months pregnant with my fourth child, so the woman really didn't what to hire me in the beginning but then she said she admired me for wanting to work this far in my pregnancy. I told her I really needed the job and she smiled at me as if she was proud of me, and she gave me the job. Of course I did my best and became a very good C.N.A. there, too. After working there for a couple of months we moved into a three bed room, two bathroom house near the railroad tracks and golf course. It was on Shady Place and I really liked it when we moved there. Things were going really well there. On December 4,

1996 my fourth and final child was born. We named her Jamila, another African name from the book which means beautiful angel. Imani's name means faith and intelligence. So then we had four children whom where all born on the fourth day of different months. We never knew what these dates meant but we thought they meant that we were soul mates and should stay together for ever. Sometimes I didn't feel that it was so because I remember early one morning, I was half asleep and T. Bell had just got up to get ready for work. He had a

Chapter 31 (Grand Theft Auto)

bowel movement and I heard him flush the toilet just before dashing out the front door because his ride was waiting outside for him. I heard the toilet attempt to flush but it didn't go down, it was stopped up because he had used to much tissue. I went to work some time after him but when I came home my son Terry, at that time was about six or seven years old and he came running to me saying, "mama, mama! You should have seen how daddy was in Quala's face screaming and yelling at her so loud that I thought he was going to hurt her. Terry said "Mama, I was so scared and Quala was, too." I went to Quala and she said, "yeah, mama, I was so scared that I wanted to scream but I thought he would hit me if I did." She said, "his face was two inches from my face and he was yelling as loud as he could saying that I stopped up the f…… toilet and that I had better clean it up as best I could." He had a habit of poking you on the forehead with his finger while he was yelling at you. He even did it to me whenever he wanted to. Terry told me that he was so afraid for Quala that he ran and got the mop to clean it up because the toilet had over flown onto the floor, but his dad wanted Quala to do it. Quala used to spend a lot of her time in her room listening to music. That was her escape from him and the hurt he used to inflict on her feelings. She was in her room when I went to talk to her. She said, "mama, he was poking me in my forehead and screaming at me so loud and with so many curse words that I was scared to do anything." When Terry came running with the mop he told him "no, not you, she's going to get it up!" And he made her get it up. I talked to T. Bell about it and he denied it as usual. "I didn't yell at he," He said. He would always say it wasn't like that, they are lying on me, but I was so used to it that I knew he was lying. Then at night he would ask me to make love as if nothing was going on while Quala cried herself to sleep. These kind of things went on for a while until I thought about leaving him, and he begged me not to and promised not to mistreat Quala anymore. After a few months I was able to get myself a car. I brought a Buick, Lesabre from one of T. Bell's friends named Erick. The car was dark blue. It was nice for me. It had air conditioning and powered windows and sunroof and everything worked properly in the car. It was a limited edition. T. Bell had received word that one of his friend's mother was in the hospital. She had had a stroke on the brain. Doctors were not expecting her to make it through the night. We got in the car and rushed to the hospital. I would probably say that we were there for about thirty minutes or less. When we got ready to leave the hospital, the car was gone. We had parked on the school property across the street from the hospital because there weren't any parking spaces at the hospital. At first I thought maybe the school security had towed my car for parking on their property. So I had T. Bell to get the security and they said that they had not towed any cars away. I was devastated, I was shocked to the point of unbelief. I started running all over the parking lot thinking that I had forgot where I had parked. I was crying uncontrollably and I was in total shock. The only trace of my car was a bunch of shattered glass In the space where my car was parked. I couldn't understand how some one could still your car in under thirty minutes. That's why I didn't want to believe that it was stolen. T. Bell just held me tight and said, "The car is gone baby, now come on, stop crying and calm down cause it's gone." I just cried my heart out as he held me. That was about 6:00 p. We called the police and made a police report, then we caught a ride home and waited. At about 12:30 am, the police called and told me that my car had been located and told me that I could go and get it from Big Ben Road. That is a very rich neighborhood. They drove my car down to the dead end of the street and into a wooded area between two huge homes. They stopped directly in front of a huge sink hole. Maybe they were hiding the car with plans to come back later or maybe they thought that it was an unsuspecting area where no one would look. It just so happened that the owner of one of the two houses they parked in between called the police and told them that there was an abandoned car near his house and gave them a description of the car. Police then called me and told me where it was. The police never went to the car to take fingerprints or anything else. When I got there my car had a shattered window, the ignition was knocked off, and they had a screwdriver laying on the front seat. They had the A.C. on high and had went through all of my CD's and was listening to something other then what I had in the CD player. They literally made them selves at home in my car. T. Bell's friend named Sammy, is the one who took us to get the car. I was glad he did because we couldn't crank the car up without the key anymore we had to use a screwdriver that the car thieves provided in order to crank the car up. Sammy showed us how to do it and that's how I had to continue to drive my car until I could afford to get the steering column fixed. I rode around for about two weeks stealing my own car. I later found out who had stolen my car; it was some of my brothers friends who just needed a ride so they just stole my car. The same boy that stole my car and admitted it and apologized to my brother not to me. He said he didn't realize that was my car or he wouldn't have stolen it. About three weeks after that this same young man went and killed another young man who was well known to all of us in the hood. He shot him and killed him about some girl. But if he had been put in jail three weeks prior for stealing my car he would not have been able to kill that boy. Things like that went on a lot in the black neighborhoods. Black on black crimes always seemed to go unnoticed. There were some good times on shady place too. Every year the super bowl was around my birthday so we would have a super bowl/ birthday party. I'd fry up large amounts of chicken wings, and loads of tuna salad, deviled eggs and sometimes meatballs or little party sandwiches. We invited all our family and friends and just had a good time. My mother was home for one of those parties which made it a little more special than the others. She had been in prison for the past two and a half years and she had time to clean herself up. She was so pretty and her skin and hair was beautiful. She had gained all her weight back and she was just a gorgeous sight to see. She had a boyfriend and his name was Willie. She had met him in the drug program. He used to smoke also but they had both turned their lives around. They both had jobs and they had an apartment together which they had obtained through the program. Sort of like a fresh start program. She was doing well and I was so proud of her. My sister and brothers were proud of her too. My mothers apartment and near by job was in Orlando, so she had to go back. I felt she was safer living in Orlando because all of her crack smoking friends were still here. I found comfort in knowing my mother was away from here and in a place where she could stay clean and live a normal life.

Chapter 32 (Fighting Like Cats an Dogs)

Trouble was still lurking at my house. After paying all the bills for the month all we had left was over was twenty-six dollars to our name. T.Bell decided that it was his money so he was going to take it and keep it. I'm not sure what we needed but I told him "you are not going to take all the money and leave me in the house with nothing". He took the money anyway and went to his friends car wash. That really pissed me off, so I went up there to the car was and told him loud and clear in front of his friends that " I can go out in the streets and sell pussy and get more money then what you took from me. He took $26 from the mother of his children. How could you even call yourself a man. A real man does not do things like that". By the time I finished saying what I had to say, he was on me. We were fighting like cats and dogs. He wanted me to shut up and get in the car but I wouldn't. I tore away from him and ran across the store and he drove over there and tried to get me into the car. We were still arguing and I was yelling insulting things at him and then I said, "I'm leaving you." He was trying to pull me into the car by my shirt but I wouldn't get in and I just took the shirt off cause he wouldn't let it go. I was running around in the parking lot in broad day light wearing a bra and no shirt. People were passing by looking out their windows at us acting like children. When we finally calmed down he gave me the money like he should have done in the beginning. That was it. I called my cousin Claudine, who was an apartment complex supervisor and explained to her about what was going on and she said she had an apartment for me but I needed to bring her a $180 quickly so she could get it ready for me. I called my friend Dee and she loaned me the money and I moved in and left him on shady place. But that didn't last long. Maybe a week if that, I can't remember exactly but he came to live with us again because he begged me and I felt sorry for him. He was cool for a while and then the bullshit started up again. My cousin Daphne, was living right across the parking lot from us. Quala spent a lot of time over there with Daphne and her kids. They were all really close and it was another way for her to stay out of her dad's sight. Daphne had three kids at that time. The first two were girls and the other, a boy. One day when I was at work, Quala called me and asked me if she could go to her friend's party that evening and I said yes. But by the time the party started, T.Bell was home. When her friends knocked on the door he let her go with them but then Quala forgot to get a jacket and ran back up upstairs to get one and he told her she couldn't go anymore. So of course she was mad and he started poking her on the forehead again and Quala said she snapped and began fighting him. He pushed her down in the closet after she had punched and kicked at him, he said. I was not there so of course I believed Quala because he always used to bother her for no reason. But I let it slide and we went on with our

134

lives again with Quala spending most of her time either in her room or at Daphne's house. I used to feel less of a woman about that stuff and I wanted out but my cousin kept saying "don't leave your husband Trece. Stay with him. He loves you." Which I knew but I didn't feel like he loved Quala the way he should have. Some nights I lay there awake wondering if Quala was crying or is she sleeping. It was the guilt I felt for letting it go on. Letting him talk me into feeling sorry for him because of how his mother treated him when he was growing up. He would always blame everything on that, and then he would cry and beg me not to leave him and I would feel sorry and stay with him. Then sometimes he would do something sweet and make me forget all about what he had done. Like once he took me to the Jamie Foxx Stand Up Comedy Show. Then after the show he had back stage passes and we were able to talk to Jamie and take pictures with him and his comedian friend, Speedy. It was wonderful, and I really enjoyed that and I still have pictures to prove it. Before we went on this trip I had to get my hair done. When I went to the beauty salon which was a very rare thing for me because I always did my own hair. I wanted to be spectacular so I went to Diane's shop. She was the best hair stylist that I knew. I had an appointment to get deep wave extensions in the back and finger waves in the front. While I was sitting there waiting, it must have been a three hour process. I watched Diane make about three hundred dollars just the time that I was there. I had already been to work for the day and I got off at 3:00 pm and I went straight to the beauty salon. This woman had been working all day before I get there and then after I left she was still working. Right then I decided that was the kind of money I wanted to make so I signed up for hair school right away, but I couldn't start school until August and it was only April. I had been thinking about a career change and this was the perfect chance. Then I got fired from my job at the nursing facility. I had to do something quick so I went and studied the CDL book because I just wanted a job with some dignity. I was tired of being called racist names as I cleaned someone's bottom who couldn't even clean their own butt but they can call you a "nigger" in a heartbeat. I got my commercial driver's license and began driving dump trucks. Just before I got my CDL, I called my dad to ask him if he could help me get the license because he owned his own underground utility construction company and he owns heavy machine equipment. I felt like it was a way for me to get experience and start working with my dad and his company but when I asked him for help he told me no. He said he didn't know what a CDL license was. So I studied hard, got my license and a job. It was a strange coincident that one day my daddy needed to have some debris hauled off one of his work cities so he called self trucking to rent a dump truck driver to haul off the old concrete. My last name let them know we were related so they sent me. My dad was so surprised to see me pull up in that huge dump truck to haul off concrete for him that he offered to take me to lunch. We went to Piccadilly's restaurant. We had lunch and talked about some things. Then he asked "You know where you got all that ambition from, don't you?" I said "No." He said "From me. That's where." I said "Yes, I believe you're right Daddy." I guess he was proud to see that I did it all by myself. It was a wonderful experience but the pay was horrible. I was making more money as a Certified Nurses Aide, plus I could work all the overtime my body could take. It was a huge pay cut, but it was so much fun. I've always had a big truck fetish and even hoped to own a RV one day, if it is in God's will. I drove dump trucks for about four months until hair school started.

The trucks were huge and sometimes when the tarp got stuck I would have to climb up the side of the truck to pull the tarp down. The trucks were old, they were big and they were slow. They only went up to seventy-five miles per hour. I burned my arm on a pipe one time trying to climb up and pull the tarp down. I was the only woman driving for this company but I learned well. Even though they gave me the most raggedy truck in the yard. I still got the job done to great satisfaction. I dumped my loads so straight that the company's would ask them to send that women back cause she knows how to drop the loads right. I got to the point where I could load my own truck using the front loader at the pit. I had a C.B. name the guys gave me, they called me Brown Sugar. It was fun hauling dirt because there were no bosses you just drive all day back and forth going to pick up dirt or to drop it off. Some times we would haul other things like shell rock and lime rock and orange sand and sometimes asphalt. I hauled asphalt to help build highway forty-four. We had to go get the asphalt and come back. Then I had to line my truck up with the paving machine so that when I dumped my asphalt it would go directly through the paver onto the road. Then they smashed the asphalt down by the roller and it becomes the new road. It was a neat process. I learned a lot from this business. I was sent on a job by myself one time way out in the back of Ormond and my truck was loaded with wet dirt because it had rained the day before and wet dirt is a lot heavier than dry dirt. So I had to back my loaded truck into a small, tight area rolling over very soft sand in order to dump this pile were it needed to be. You have to figure out how to position the truck to dump the load exactly where they wanted it or they would not be asking you to come back. I was slowly backing in and I could feel the truck sinking into the soft sand so I had to hurry and dump the truck and then I tried to pull out. I was stuck. I had to rock the truck back and forth then I put the shift differential lock on and put it in low gear and I came up out of that soft dirt by myself. That took experience and brains to get that truck out without calling for help and I did it. Boy was I proud of myself.

Chapter 33 (Hair School)

Then before I knew it was time for hair school. I had decided I wanted to change my whole career. It was the first time that I was proud of myself for doing something as positive as going to college. People don't think of hair school as college but it is. When I started school is when we moved in the projects, and when I starting letting the Lord in my life. My husband's grandmother Earnestine Robinson had just past and I was able to inherit her bible. I started going to church and praying everyday. I started a relationship with God, but it wasn't a strong relationship yet. I was going to school everyday I was studying and passing all my tests and had met some good people and we became good friends. One was Michelle Harris and the other was Teresa Bishop. When school was over it was a sad day cause we knew we wouldn't see each other any more cause we had our own families and that alone can cause distance in friendships. We all cried on the last day and said our goodbyes. We all passed our state board test but I think I'm the only one who went ahead and worked in the field. I think Michelle and Teresa are doing other things. After I got out I started working at Cut Master's barbershop. This was in the year 2002. I started school in

2000 and finished one year later. I graduated with honors, past my state board test and got my cosmetology license. My cousins husband named Oliver works there so I asked him, "could you make a lot of money cutting hair?" He said, " yes." Then I asked him, " do you think that Derrick, the owner, would give me a job there?" And he said, " yes." I asked Derrick and he said, " sure." He informed that it was a Christian atmosphere and everybody in there were their own boss. He also informed me of the weekly booth rental and that it was due in advance. I accepted all his conditions and began working there right away. I'm thankful that it is a Christian atmosphere because it helped me to stop saying so many curse words. Then I started singing in the choir, which is something I always wanted to do. Derrick is the pastor of his own church located directly behind the barbershop. It is a nice size barbershop. It has twelve stations. It is a great place to work and everyone who works there is blessed. All of the barbers that work there are really good people and their names are Oliver, Tyrone, Derrick, Darcia , Robert, Mike, Tiny, Gail, Robbie and myself. At first I was afraid because I did not know how to cut black men's hair. Oliver showed me the basics of a fade but Tyrone showed me how to put that flavor on it. At first I was visibly shaking when it came time for me to do a fade. I used to come home from work sometimes almost in tears because I thought I was never going to learn. Some days I would come home with only thirty-five dollars for the whole day and T.Bell would joke about it saying "Quala makes more money than you!" It used to hurt my feelings cause all day at work Derrick and his wife used to take all the customers cause I was not aggressive back then. They would cut really fast to hurry and get the next customer also. All the while knowing that I had to pay them booth rental and I had to race them to pay them. This went on every day, even on Fridays when all of us had to pay booth rent. It is a very cut throat business and it used to bother me very bad but Tyrone Brooks, the best barber I know, who works right next to me, told me to take my time and do each and every hair cut to the best of my ability and the people will come back to me every time. That is exactly what I did and sure enough I started building a clientele of people who stuck with me no matter what. We've had a lot of fun days in the shop too. Half the barbers and half the customers love to crack on each other and tell jokes. There's always something to laugh about in the shop. Sometimes the jokes would last for hours, or even days, but no curse words in the shop. From working in a Christian atmosphere I got closer to the church and ultimately closer to God. The customers that stick with me mean a lot to me and I go out of my way to please them. One family in particular is the Parks family. John and Brittney Parks have been some die hard customers and I really appreciate them and their two beautiful children. May God continue to bless them.

Chapter 34 (Back at New St. James)

After singing in the choir at Derrick's church I wanted to sing in a big church choir so I went back to the church I was married in and stayed there. The name of that church is New St. James Missionary Baptist Church located on Laura street in Daytona Beach, Fl. Where Jesus is Lord and you are loved. I joined their choir and became a member of the church again. The pastor now is Craig Robinson and what a wonderful pastor he is. He has a way of taking Gods word and making it ever so clear and understandable. He has been there for my family in great times of need. His prayers have been so genuine and so deeply rooted from his soul that you know automatically that is an anointed man of God. When my son received his first car ever, at the age of seventeen, he decided to get with some of his friends and go rob five convenient stores. My husband and I had no clue that he was doing any of this because he was going to school and coming home by curfew every day so we don't know when he was doing these things. One day my sister called me and said, "Trece I just saw Terry on the news wanted for string of robberies from Putnam county to Volusia county." She said, "they had the car on the news too. I called Terry immediately and told him to come home now. In about fifteen minutes he was home. I told him what his aunt told me and he said that she was lying and that he had never been there and it must be someone who looks like him. Some how he convinced me that it was not him. I waited up all night to see the news but it never came on in Daytona. My sister lives in Jacksonville and that's where it aired. After a couple of weeks had passed and they had not come to get him I really believed it must not be him cause he's not hiding. He goes to school everyday and they had not come to get him yet. When they did come to get him they got him from school cause they said that he might have a weapon. It was our anniversary, December 17, 2008. We were getting ready to go have a nice day together. We had brought matching outfits and we made plans for an all day event. Then the phone ranged. It was Terry's principal telling us that the Holly Hill police had just arrested Terry and they had a warrant there was nothing he could do to stop them. I started crying uncontrollably because I knew what my sister said was true. A few minutes later the phone rang again, it was the police. They said we need you to come down and get Terry to cooperate. They told me that they would put in a good word for my son at the state attorney office if he confessed. I've never been through any thing like this before so I made him confess. They never did put in a good word for my son but what they did for his confession was put in the paper that he ratted out his co-defendant and blamed everything on him, and that was not true. Terry told them and I was right there, that he himself walked in with the gun and said, " I'm not here to hurt you just give me the money." The fact that that surveillance camera showed two people without masks and the Volusia county school officials told police who both of these boys were is the only reason why Terry had to say yes it was both of us. That's not ratting your co-defendant out that's simply confessing after being I.D. from both schools and the pictures. Our pastor Craig L. Robinson was there every step of the way. He had congregational prayers for my son. He also went to every court hearing my son had and spoke on Terry's behalf. He even went out to the jail house to visit Terry. That is a true Pastor, a man after God's own heart. I love him for who he is and for all that he has done for my family. Pastor Robinson was even there for me when I had an accident and had to get titanium in my spine to replace some bad discs. He led the church in prayer for me also. I was on my death bed when I had that operation. All kinds of complications could have come up but through the prayers, God took care of me and nursed my back to health. After the surgery I couldn't get up and work for about a month and a half and I had to sleep in a neck brace the whole time. I was at my weakest point at that time because I couldn't provide for my family. T.Bell was doing the best he could but we were on the brink of starvation and Derrick and his wife still wanted me to pay booth rent but I couldn't pay any of my bills at that time so he and his wife agreed for him to call me and tell me I had to get my stuff out of his barbershop if I couldn't pay my booth rent. So my family got my things and Derrick moved someone else into my station. Just like that, after 5 years of employment . It hurt me, for them to kick me while I was down but it also made me stronger. When I came back I concentrated on my haircuts, built up my cliental, and gained authority over my emotions. Things just fell into place and got better and better. I spoke to the Pastor about these things going on at my job and he said "You know, sometimes God will close one door just to open another door for you. He has given you a talent, he has provided you with a beautiful home." He said, "I think you can cut hair in your garage and save yourself some money." To me, it was a great idea. I wondered if it was a message from God, and so the thought has been in my mind every day. God did bless us with a beautiful home after we let him into our lives. We only rent the home, but I have faith that one day we'll be able to buy it and own it. I learned to let go and let God handle things and it brings me so much peace and joy just to know that all I really need is Jesus. Our home is a four bedroom, two full bathroom home. And it has an in ground pool, a two car garage, and a huge front and backyard. I love it and I thank God everyday for it. Coming from the projects, to this big house was like going from rags to riches. My kids finally had their own room, and they were over joyed to live in a safer and more courteous neighborhood. While living in the projects, our apartment and our cars had been burglarized and T.Bell almost lost his life. Some guys were outside shooting nine millimeters and when T.Bell went to get the kids inside, one of the bullets hit the pole, and by it being an iron pole, the bullet shattered and a lot of fragments went into his back. That's when we knew it was time to get out of there. Two weeks later we moved into this home and have been here for the last 5 years. I have a flourishing garden and plenty of plants. My front porch is covered in God's glorious plants. Everything I plant grows, so I guess I have a green thumb. Funny thing is, my grandfather, who I didn't even know I had until the age of thirty, came to my house and cleaned out a lot of grass from the yard and started me this garden. He planted collard greens for me, tomatoes, squash ,eggplants, green peppers, and banana peppers. It was so special. Even more special is the fact that he was ninety-one years old when he made this garden for me. He told me that the closet place to talk to God is your garden. I began talking to God in my garden. Sometimes about joyful things, sometimes about sad things. Sometimes just to talk in general, nothing special at all. I had gained a grandfather, who taught me how to garden. My daddy had never talked about his father to me , so therefore I thought I didn't have a granddad. I got close to him in just a small amount of time from our frequent visits. I became his barber and sometimes I would fix him some lunch as he worked in my garden. It took him about two weeks to dig everything out and fertilize the ground because of his age but when the job was done, it was so beautiful. Talking to God in my garden helped me deal with a lot of things in my life. Like when my cousin Daphne and Michelle had a terrible car accident that broke Michelle's neck and claimed Daphne's life. She was thrown from the truck and was killed instantly. We never had a chance to say goodbye. It was such a devastation that I could not pick myself up off the ground. I could only sit there and pull up grass with all my might from the ground. It felt like I couldn't breath, the shock was so great. Again Pastor Robinson was there. He spoke at her funeral because I asked him to. He took the time out of his busy schedule and came to speak a kind word and to ease our hearts and minds by letting us know that to be absent fro the body is to be present with the Lord. I know she is in heaven with God and her mother and our grandmother are all there too and their all happy. I have learned to play the piano through the teachings of a great woman I met by the name of Casey Baker. She started teaching me to play the piano after I told T.Bell that I wanted to play for my church. I wanted to be just like Pastor Robinson's wife who is the director of our choir. Someday I hope to be able to play the piano in church just like she does. I have already learned to play When The Saints Go Marching In, and Standing In The Need of Prayer but I'm still learning. I know that if I study hard that God will give me the talent of a great piano player one day. Sometimes I stand in my garden and thank God for all the wonderful things and all the blessings that he has rained down on me and my family. He has brought me a mighty long way. Through great trails and tribulations, and I know it's not over yet. God has a plan for me. After being a barber for a few years I realized I was ruining a lot of shoes from falling debris and hair. When you're a barber, the powder falls on your shoes, the disinfectant spray falls on your shoes, the oil sheen falls on your shoes and then all the hair falls on your shoes. When the day is over you have stuff plastered on your shoes. I decided to invent shoe protectors. I went to the store, purchased some materials and made what I call "Attachable Shoe covers" and sent pictures of them to an invention company. They loved the idea. In March of 2010, I was issued a patent from the united states patent office. That was truly a blessing from God to go from an idea to an actual invention. I hope to someday be in the Black History Books like all the other recognized black inventors. It is such a great feeling that it has inspired me to tell somebody about the goodness of the Lord and all his mighty blessings. The best way for me to tell the world is by writing this book. It does not matter how low you may think you are, God can pick you up and change you from trash to treasure. He has turned my life around completely and all because I chose to trust in him and have faith in him through all things, for there is nothing new on the earth. God can do all things and through Christ all things are possible. So I say to all my brothers and my sisters let go and let God.

The end

Dedication Page

This book is dedicated to my sweet Grand Mother Rosa B. Tiller.

She died at the age of 82 and she was a great woman of God. May God rest your humble soul.

This book is also dedicated to my closest cousin Daphne Ledbetter. A faithful mom and good friend and confidant. May God rest your beautiful soul in peace and harmony for all eternity.

And last but not least in dedication to my dear Aunt Lillie Mae to God be the glory.

I will let my light shine for all the world to see.
Author: L'trece Ann Worsham